Clint Eastwood

Vs.

The Rainbow

David Womack

✳✳✳✳✳✳✳✳✳✳✳✳✳✳✳

Clint Eastwood vs. the Rainbow

Racism, Misogyny, Homophobia and other Cinematic Foolishness

Flying Public Press
1959 45th Ave.
San Francisco, CA. 94116

Thanks:
Geoffrey Ellis for the cover;
Billie, Lily, Ron, Marsha, Glenn

Goddesses in the band
The Dream
Time and
The Word. Yes!

CONTENTS

Clint Eastwood vs. The Rainbow

In the late fifties and early sixties movie culture was undergoing major changes. In retrospect, it's hard to believe the motion picture industry's censorship arm - the Hays Code - which had been in place since 1930, was just beginning to be challenged. By 1968 the Code was abolished, freeing up story content for a movie audience starved for a more free-ranging cinema.

Movie fever was rising. Springing up and spreading to cities across the USA, repertory movie theaters mixed overlooked B-movie gems, oddball cult sensations and an increasing number of foreign films.

At the same time, movies were becoming more widely available for television. By the mid-sixties, *Halliwell's Film Guide* became the prototype for film encyclopedias; hundreds upon hundreds of films were synopsized and rated. Deprived film fans who came of age during this time may recall pouring over their weekly *TV Guide,* circling the most interesting films they could find - sniffing them out from mid-day to the early hours of dawn in fetishistic delight.

Film-making classes were becoming a standardized part of college curriculum and would spawn a future wave of talented filmmakers. Film criticism was in its heyday. Inspired by an unbounded love for American movies, French film critics began assigning overriding "authorship" of movies, not to the story writers, but to film directors. The "auteur" theory was born. Movies were no longer the artistic fermentation of writers, actors, producers, designers and technicians; instead, the most potent films were single-handed visionary orchestrations guided by the film director. The auteurists posited the film-director as the only person who could parlay the vast chaos of film-making into the single-minded glory of personal art - everybody else's role was subsidiary. American film-goers may have had favorite actors, or favorite genres but, with exceptions like Alfred Hitchcock whose personality became linked to his movies through a certain amount of PR acumen and an obviously idiosyncratic style, the directorial presence in films was overlooked. In a movie like *Strawberry Blonde,* a buoyant 1941 romantic comedy taking place in turn-of-the-20th-century America, audiences would have been entertained by James Cagney, Olivia de Havilland, Rita Hayworth; they would have heard the songs "The Band Played On," "Bill Bailey," "Meet Me in St Louis, Louie," "Wait Till the Sun Shines Nellie" and "Love Me and the World is Mine." They may have swooned over the costumes by Orry-Kelly, and laughed at the repartee provided by Julius and Philip Epstein (Cagney: "That's the kind of hairpin I am."). The film also boasted cinematography by the esteemed James Wong Howe.

But the French auteur critics mostly noticed Raoul Walsh, the movie's director. French critics would point out Walsh's consistency in a career that extended from the silent movie era to the early sixties and included *Roaring Twenties, They Drive by Night, High Sierra, They Died with Their Boots On, Gentleman Jim, White Heat, A Lion is in the Streets* and *Gun Fury.* They would point out Walsh's technical adeptness at handling action films and the naked vulnerability of his male action heroes.

Clint Eastwood began his rise to stardom in the early sixties. His move to director would begin at the end of the decade and it would seem logical that the new film zeitgeist might have influenced his work. Instead, as both actor and director, the changes noted above had little impact. If anything, Eastwood was a conservative throwback. His acting style would show little emotional expansion throughout the years. His rise as director was oddly casual; he didn't have the fever of a cultist or the focus on technical style of the film school graduates. For a large number of films, he was content to come in under budget and turn a profit. Eastwood's ambitions were muted; he belonged to a less reflective age.

Drafted into the army in 1951, Eastwood somehow missed out on being shipped to Korea. Instead, he found himself stationed at Fort Ord on California's coast near Monterey. His duties included teaching swimming classes and running a movie projector. Among his army buddies were future movie stars like David Jansen (*The Fugitive*) and Martin Milner (*Adam-12*). When Eastwood's tour of duty ended, he landed in Los Angeles. He worked odd jobs, tried his luck as an actor and appears to have taken up drama classes at the advice of unimpressed Hollywood agents. By 1954, he was doing screen tests.

Eastwood's acting career started fitfully in the mid-fifties with a smattering of bit parts in film and television. His big break and his first impression on America's consciousness came when he was chosen for the role of Rowdy Yates in the dusty cowboy cattle-driving television series *Rawhide* which would run for 8 seasons from January 1959 to January 1966. It was on set that Eastwood observed first-hand the mechanics of the film business and the craft of putting together film narratives. Eastwood was with *Rawhide* so long he began to feel worthy of directing an episode, but his requests for the director's chair never materialized.

Eastwood would be a different kind of director than Francis Ford Coppola, Steven Spielberg, Martin Scorsese, or even a closer peer like Robert Altman who also learned film technique while directing television Westerns. Eastwood was not art conscious; to some degree, his reactionary conservative inclinations made him antagonistic to "cinematic art." Eastwood eventually cruised into the director's chair influenced not by film theories or cold technology or immersion in ideas about film-making, but by the simplicity and swiftness of television production: its workmanship and frugality; its ability to fill up screen time with ideas that pulled in money.

Even though some practitioners of the auteur theory would eventually be kind to Eastwood, Eastwood seemed a bit oblivious to the concept. A chapter of Marc Eliot's biography on Eastwood is entitled "From Actor to Auteur," but the assessment seems Eliot's rather than Eastwood's. For instance, Eliot notes that when director Donald Siegel was suggested as director for an early Eastwood acting vehicle (*Coogan's Bluff* in 1968), Eastwood didn't know who Siegel was and had to screen Siegel's classic 1956 film *Invasion of the Body Snatchers* before he felt comfortable with the choice. It is unlikely that Coppola and Altman, or youngsters like Martin Scorsese who directed his first feature in 1967, were unfamiliar with Siegel's work.

Andrew Sarris, a film critic who helped formulate the auteur theory in America in the sixties would eventually write positive reviews for several Eastwood-directed movies. His book *The American Cinema: Directors and Directions 1929 - 1968* was an important early attempt to critique and rank works by individual directors. His summaries often carried the lilt of great quotes. Here he is on John Ford, Howard Hawks and Raoul Walsh:

"If the heroes of Ford are sustained by tradition, and the heroes of Hawks by professionalism, the heroes of Walsh are sustained by nothing more than a feeling for adventure. The Fordian hero knows why he is doing something even if he doesn't know how. The Hawksian hero knows how to do what he is doing even if he doesn't know why. The Walshian hero is less interested in the why or the how than in the what."

Sarris offered insights on the work of both the most original and consistent of directors, as well as the most marginal of stylists - from a master like Max Ophuls ("This is the ultimate meaning of Ophulsian camera movement: time has no stop. Montage tends to suspend time in the limbo of abstract images, but the moving camera records inexorably the passage of time, moment by moment.") - to inconsistent directors like William Dieterle ("Dieterle was around on the set when many interesting things happened over the years, and it is reasonable to assume that he had something to do with them."). It is somewhere between Sarrisian extremes that the auteur theory would have to contemplate Clint Eastwood as an artist.

****

The movie critic Pauline Kael, on the other hand, was an anarchistic American rebel throwing bombs at films, film critics and film theories everywhere. Given the length of her diatribes, she may have been partially inspired by being paid per word, but she certainly didn't do it while lacking in passion: in the early sixties, Kael was given plenty of room to pontificate in periodicals like *Kulchur*, *Sight and Sound*, *Film Quarterly*, *Atlantic Monthly*, and *Moviegoer*. She would state: "... one of [the critics] most important functions: perceiving what is original and important in *New* work and helping others to see." Kael suggested movies were to be viewed strictly on a case-by-case basis - not as some kind of formulaic directorial continuum. Every movie was a work unto itself and succeeded or failed based on viewable virtues.

At worst, Kael seemed compelled to laden the simplest of films with heavy arguments, collating any recent knowledge she may have picked up into any stray film review she happened to be writing at the time. When Kael laid into a film it could seem so expansive as to court the ridiculous - it may be "just a movie, Pauline" - but for Kael the rise and fall of civilization was entwined in personal views on everything from *Last Year at Marienbad* to *West Side Story*. On the maximal side, she could always impress you with her knowledge of source material - from *War and Peace* to *The Seagull*. On the minimal side of things, opening credits did not sneak by while Kael was putting butter on her popcorn. No woefully misused soundtrack would lilt away needlessly without being called out. No bit actor could hide lazily in the shadows escaping derision, but no sublime sliver of acting truth would remain neglected. If a film was a hack job, she expected it to carry some sense of joy. If a film was tackling a big subject, she expected it to live up to the attempt. Big ideas and little ideas were met with the same critical ferocity. Either way, she wanted to be entertained.

If Kael was well ahead of her time, it wasn't just in a theoretical sense, but in an observational, empirical sense. She made other reviewers seem old-fashioned, pedestrian, sleepy, careless, venal. For instance, in a review of the 1961 English film *Victim*, in which the unusual plot involves the murder and blackmail of gay men, she notes:

> "A number of reviewers were uneasy about the thesis that consenting adults should be free from legal prosecution for their sex habits; they felt that if homosexuality were not a crime it would spread."

She quoted a *Times* reviewer who stated:

> "But what seems at first an attack on extortion seems at last a coyly sensational exploitation of homosexuality as a theme - and what's more offensive, an implicit approval of homosexuality as a practice. Almost all of the deviates in the film are fine fellows .... Nowhere does the film suggest that homosexuality is a serious (but often curable) neurosis that attacks the biological basis of life itself."

Ultimately Kael would tag *Victim* as "moderately amusing," the film itself a footnote to some righteous cultural observations.

Kael was hard on movies, hard on actors and hard on movie critics. She had no use for the "superlatives" style of hyped-up film criticism - "this movie is gangbusters" - "the highest achievement of cinema this decade," - "another masterpiece,' - "the best movie so far this year," etc. Kael served as a brake on the worst intentions of a good many interesting critics and she spared us the horrid puns. She parleyed with Bosley Crowther (*New York Times*), Stanley Kauffman (*New Republic*), Dwight MacDonald (Esquire), Andrew Sarris and many others.

Kael was skeptical of the auteur theory. In a long article entitled "Circles and Squares" published in *Film Quarterly* in 1963 she laid out her problems:

"... it may be necessary to point out to auteur critics that repetition without development is decline."

"When a famous director makes a good movie, we look at the movie, we don't think about the director's personality; when he makes a stinker we notice his familiar touches because there's not much else to watch."

Unlike many of the auteur critics and superlatives critics, Pauline Kael was not a fan of Clint Eastwood. According to Marc Eliot's Eastwood biography, Kael bothered Eastwood enough that she was a subject of discussion with his psychiatrist. Eliot also quotes a *Video* magazine interview in which Eastwood states: "[Kael] found an avenue that was going to make her a star. I was just one of the subjects, among many, that helped her along the way."

It's incontestable that Kael didn't single out Eastwood for particular scorn - he put his movies out and they were there to be reviewed. Kael would not back down even when discussing the work of directors for whom she expressed great admiration - Robert Altman, Martin Scorsese, Brian DePalma, Sam Peckinpah. She might have high praise for Altman's *McCabe and Mrs. Miller*, but she detested *Brewster McCloud* and *Fool for Love*. She suggested Scorsese was in decline as early as *After Hours* in 1985. Although she considered Sam Peckinpah a friend, she thought the best actors in the Peckinpah film *Convoy* were the trucks. ("The trucks give the performances in this movie.")

Kael's problem with Eastwood resided in what she thought film-making could be at its best. If the auteur theory was thorough enough to encompass and categorize almost every director, then Clint Eastwood could fit in somewhere, and inclusion itself is somewhat of an elevation. But Kael needed something sturdier to smash her critical stick against and Eastwood's movies barely sufficed. When Eastwood puzzles over how Kael, whom he mistakenly called a "neo-feminist," could fall head over heels for Bernardo Bertolucci's *Last Tango in Paris* with its misogynist and misanthropic male lead played by Marlon Brando, he disingenuously suggests that *Tango* is the same kind of movie he makes; that Bertolucci's depiction of an American's misogyny and misanthropy was the same as the misogyny and misanthropy Eastwood himself expressed in his films.

Eastwood suggested that Kael hated his films because of their "maleness." In actuality, Kael insisted that "maleness" encompass some sort of movie-making fervor, some emotional consideration, some aesthetic / artistic uniqueness. If a film is violent, shouldn't the film express *ideas* about violence? Eastwood may have thought Kael was picking on him, but she was always sifting through his ideas, looking beyond the audience-pleasing sensationalism, trying to find something to talk about, seldom finding anything that necessitated much comment.

Certainly, Kael was culturally aware of the ramifications of "maleness" and "violence." Action-packed films offered an immersive quality that she found exhilarating or a rottenness that she found stupefying. She foretold the death of the old-style Western early on:

> "Of all art forms, movies are most in need of having their concepts of heroism undermined. ... In recent years John Ford, particularly, has turned the Western into an almost static pictorial genre, a devitalized, dehydrated form which is "enriched" with pastoral beauty and evocative nostalgia for a simple, heroic way of life. The clichés we retain from childhood movies ... have been awarded the status of myth, and directors have been making infatuated tributes to the myths of our old movies."

On the other hand, she considered Akira Kurosawa's Japanese film *The Seven Samurai* a masterpiece:

> "Fighting itself is the subject of *The Seven Samurai* - an epic on violence and action, a raging, sensuous work of such overpowering immediacy that it leaves you both exhilarated and exhausted."

But this doesn't mean *The Seven Samurai* received a free pass:

> "*The Seven Samurai* is the kind of action-packed, thundering-hooves, death-dealing spectacle which is considered a man's picture. I propose to turn this hazard to my advantage by suggesting that the weaknesses of the film are closely linked to the limitations of the virile, masculine genre."

She would cite a problem with *Samurai* that suggested the problems she had with Eastwood's character portrayals:

> "When violence itself becomes the theme, when it is treated with such extraordinary range that we are caught up in what is literally an epic of action, we need protagonists commensurate with the pictorial grandeur."

If Kael's view of action and violence seems too negatively discerning, you can look on the back of every Clint Eastwood DVD ever released and find a host of positive quotes from, among others, Peter Travers, Richard Corliss, Gene Shalit, Jack Kroll and Vincent Canby - and you will find them on both the best and the worst of Eastwood's films. The elements of commercial compromise that exist in reviews by the superlatives writers can probably be overstated but that doesn't mean compromise isn't involved. As an example: this remark from the journalist Seymour Hersh (*TLS* June 1, 2018) who in 2003 interviewed Bashar al-Assad, the Syrian president already known for his penchant for torture and the use of chemical weapons:

"One rarely discussed issue among journalists has to do with access; we of course tend to like those senior officials and leaders, such as Assad, who grant us interviews and speak openly with us. But access inevitably provokes ethical dilemmas."

If an esteemed and established journalist has problems keeping proper objectivity with feigned politeness from a sociopath then one can see a problem arising when the celebrities one is dealing with are charming actors or actresses or directors who might arrive with a peck on the cheek, a warm handshake, movie tickets and an autograph that can be sold on *eBay*. There are times to ride easy on a popular artist you or your publisher might need for a lucrative interview or a major cover story and there are times when you can take an opportunity to tell them what you really think.

Regional, political and cultural apprehensions of films play a role as well. The first-string newspaper critic isn't going to last long if he pisses off his film-going readership *all* of the time. What plays badly in California might not play as badly in small town Alabama. A film that might get a down-side three-star review in the *San Francisco Chronicle* might be fine for the readership of the conservative *Weekly Standard*. As the Pete Seeger song suggests - there is a time to balance the last tepidly negative review of a director's movie with your new tepidly positive review. Hopefully some kind of objective standards will prevail to give credence to the general purpose of film criticism over the long haul. Audience beware.

****

The title of Marc Eliot's biography - *Clint Eastwood: American Rebel* - is a misnomer. Clint Eastwood is an American *conservative* and his filmic instincts and story-telling instincts are based on cinematic conservatism. His initial impetus with his production company, *Malpaso*, was to make financially successful films firmly under his guidance. Rebellion against money-making interests would be counter-productive. Art was ancillary.

Would Eastwood have had anything to sell through *Malpaso* if he had not been blessed in his early career with strong directors like Sergio Leone and Don Siegel? The work of these directors gave Clint Eastwood the brands (*The Man With No Name* and *Dirty Harry*) that would establish his viability as an audience pleasing presence and as a successful producer. Leone's *Fistful of Dollars* (1964), *For a Few Dollars More* (1965) and *The Good, the Bad and the Ugly* (1966) were prime examples of the Italian produced "spaghetti" Westerns and Eastwood fit perfectly into those outsized cowboy boots and fulsome ponchos. Siegel's *Coogan's Bluff* and *Dirty Harry* were hard-boiled action flicks with masterful depictions of true crime grit. These movies provided the archetypes that Eastwood would rely on to jumpstart and intermittently recharge his directing career.

Playing "The Man with No Name" required an impressive physical presence but little acting range. As Sergio Leone pointed out when comparing Eastwood to Robert De Niro: "They don't even belong to the same profession ... Eastwood moves like a sleepwalker between explosions and hails of bullets, and he is always the same." Donald Siegel would use Eastwood in much the same way in *Coogan's Bluff* (1968), *Two Mules for Sister Sara* (1970), *Dirty Harry* (1971) and *Escape from Alcatraz* (1979). Although it's often assumed that Eastwood's general demeanor was perfect for Leone's films (they made lots of money), it's hard not to detect the back-handed compliment in Leone's remarks. The last half of *The Good, The Bad and the Ugly* has some visual delights, and it's fun to watch Eli Wallach and Lee Van Cleef go through their strenuously sweaty, shifty-eyed, crying, chortling, mouth-spitting, mud-spattered paces; Eastwood looks like he just wandered over from the STAR trailer after a shower with a clean set of cowboy clothes. The stock and trade of Eastwood's acting style is made with flimsy threads:

1. Iron face
2. Tics of cheek muscles
3. Squinting of eyes, like the sun just hit him
4. Stern glare
5. Derisive swallowed guffaw - never really a laugh
6. Quick teeth-clenched grimace
7. One-sided half-smile
8. Almost furrowed brow
9. Cigar (in Italy Eastwood was referred to as "El Cigarillo.")

Eastwood was also "The Man with No Voice." There isn't much there: a gruff mumble that never completely escapes his chest, a feeling that words are not his preferred mode of expression, almost a vocal shyness, or even a vocal embarrassment - like he is trying to hide, not his feelings, but his actual speaking voice. This is fine when he is playing a

14

silent, gun-toting mysterioso but pretty useless when playing a disc jockey, a college professor, a smitten lover, a talkative movie director icon or a country-western singer. Eastwood avoids verbal dexterity in his films - as a script doctor he's known for scissoring out large swaths of his own dialogue. Perhaps correlated to this is his tin ear for character dialogue in general and the irritating, unconstrained pitch at which many of his actors launch their line readings.

Given his preferred choice of material it is possible Eastwood has seen himself as a later-day hard-boiled director in the manner of Siegel, Phil Karlson (*Fury, Kansas City Confidential, Phoenix City Story*), Anthony Mann (*Raw Deal, Winchester '73, Men in War*), or Budd Boetticher (*Tall T, Buchanan Rides Alone, Rise and Fall of Legs Diamond*). Unfortunately, Eastwood's "action-packed" flicks are not particularly good examples of true crime sordidness, prickly film noir sensibility, or Boetticher-styled meditations on morality. His films lack the struggling desperation and the anarchic vividness of the gruff and idiosyncratic character actors that enliven many of their films (some Eastwood exceptions - *High Plains Drifter* and *Unforgiven*). More importantly, for Siegel, Mann, Karlson, and for Eastwood peers like Altman, Scorsese and William Friedkin, the horrid consequences of violent acts, abusive bullying, passive-aggressive criminality, psychotic vigilantism are thematically and morally recognized, considered, *registered*. For the most part, Eastwood's films are oblivious to the effects of violence. Many of them are like super-hero films with nasty minds. The super-hero is a little bit off - he's a racist and/or a sexist. He's a superhero - he never loses; as a result, the dramatic impulses of realism are seldom present. When Eastwood's heroes get beat up - a few film-minutes later it doesn't look like the beating hurt all that much (in comparison: in Roman Polanski's *Chinatown*, Jack Nicholson's Jake Gettis gets his nose sliced and he wears a bloody nose bandage for a long stretch of film-time and it looks very tender when Faye Dunaway's Evelyn Mulwray touches it; in Altman's *The Long Goodbye* Elliott Gould's Philip Marlowe is badly beaten and has his nose and eye bandaged afterwards - you can feel how much he hurts).

There are a lot of ways to view a director's work, but there is a limit to what a director offers that is viewable. Technical accomplishment, the bedrock of many directors on the low side of the auteurist spectrum, is problematic because Eastwood often glorified his low budgets, his fast shooting-schedule, his tendency to defer to his stable of technicians and craftsmen as he kept his eye on the monetary return. Financially speaking this was fine, on an artistic level it is perhaps the sin of pride in ephemeral glories. Cinematic ambition is not the forte of a director who purportedly puts golfing and movie-making on roughly the same level.

Eastwood's direction of actors may have been stunted because he avoided them for a large part of his career in favor of putting himself in the spotlight. Eastwood does not hold the screen like Chaplin, Brando, Streep, McQueen, Jeff Bridges or even Charles Bronson. Yet most of his movies are bereft of good foils. To state that Eastwood is just a "different type of actor" marginalizes his acting into negligence.

Emotion is seldom present because Eastwood films in general are not emotionally oriented, they are action / sensationalism oriented. His action flicks are usually choices of convenience, he's looking for a slight variation, another money-making repetition, not a strenuous stretch of the imagination.

Until *Academy Award* recognition started being tossed his way - I'd peg it at about 30 years into his career around the time of *Mystic River* - an Eastwoodian "aesthetics of cinema" barely registered in his films except as a negative default. By the time he became slightly art-conscious, it was too little too late. At that point, Eastwood shifted to another fairly simple business model: he began removing himself from the center of action; he began to rely on a more distinguished pool of acting talent - from Sean Penn to Meryl Streep; and he began to consider screenplays that gave a few actors time to shine as drama replaced melodrama. As the films became more endurable, Eastwood's directing personality receded further into the background - moving from rank to invisible. In considering Eastwood's final resting place in the auteurist catalogue one has to reckon with a host of lurid, creepy waitresses, dead black friends, long fist fights with no consequences, mindless car crashes, violence without any apprehension of what violence entails, and a late attempt (ultimately abandoned) to turn a few of those things around.

It may be that Eastwood was hopelessly behind-the-times the minute he stepped up to the camera in 1971 - that he was already irrelevant, out of step with everything around him, perhaps even epitomizing the worst of what had come before him. In retrospect, Donald Siegel's mentorship of Eastwood seems to have been of the least philosophical kind: you gotta wake up in the morning, find a script, hire some actors and go out and point the camera.

Racism, Misogyny, Homophobia & Other Cinematic Foolishness

High Plains Drifter – 1973

Eastwood's second film (after *Play Misty for Me*) is a nice place to start because it illustrates the fast-spoiled potential of his efforts at directing.

High Plains Drifter is a recasting of Leone's man-with-no-name Westerns but with a difference. There are none of the slippery areas between good, bad or ugly that cast the Leone films with shades of dark-hearted humanism. In *High Plains Drifter* everybody is bad and ugly. This was Eastwood's first film with Henry Bumstead on board as art director and Bumstead's work is beautiful in a very simplistic way. Eastwood dragged Bumstead out to Mono Lake, California and the film crew built a town from scratch. The result is a rickety desert ghost town that looks ready to blow away in a dry wind. This town is called Lago. Lago's inhabitants are baked rotten like dead desert meat.

Ernest Tidyman (author of the *Shaft* series of books and *Academy Award* winner for his *French Connection* screenplay) wrote the script. Tidyman squeezes every drop of civility, sentiment, and good intentions out of his characters. They are devils - devious, corrupt, self-serving, murderous.

A gun-toting stranger rides into Lago. As he sits in a barber's chair waiting for a shave, three gunmen taunt him. Gunplay ensues and he dispatches them.

The stranger's second act of manliness: a woman (Mariana Hill) insults him when she bumps into him on the street, so he drags her into a horse stable and rapes her. For a rape scene - it's not the best played. There's both a "she-deserved-it" and a "she-wanted-it" flavor in the acting and the action. I'm sort of speechless on how to access the scene – the woman is supposed to blend in with the rest of the motley characters I suppose, but something is missing in the subtext (perhaps because there is no subtext).

The Sheriff of Lago, Sam Shaw (Walter Barnes), is disturbed that his hired hands have been killed, but he offers the stranger the job of protecting the town. The stranger is told that the previous lawman, Marshall Jim Duncan (seen in flashbacks and played by Buddy Van Horn), discovered the town leaders were involved in a crooked mining business. As a result, the mayor (Stefan Gierasch) and local businessmen hired the outlaw Carlin Brothers (Don Vadis and Anthony James) and fellow gunman Stacey Bridges (Geoffrey Lewis) to kill Marshall Duncan. In plain sight of the citizens of Lago, the Marshall was whipped to death in the street. The townsfolk then betrayed the three gunmen and sent them to prison. Now they are out and riding back to Lago to take revenge.

The stranger accepts the job and takes up residence at a local hotel after he forces everybody else out. He appoints the most incompetent of the townsfolk, a barbershop worker named Mordecai (Billy Curtis), as the new mayor.

The old mayor and his cronies don't trust the stranger and various attempts are made on his life. Most of the gunplay is handled with entertaining dexterity. The stranger pretends to assist the townsfolk in learning how to defend themselves, but abandons them at the last minute, leaving the

Carlin Brothers and Bridges to come in and kill the people who double-crossed them.

The stranger then returns and whips one Carlin brother to death, whips and hangs the other, then shoots Bridges dead in the street. The town burns. As the stranger rides away, he passes Marshall Duncan's tombstone (suggesting that he was perhaps Duncan returned from the grave). Livening up the various connivances are Verna Bloom, Robert Donner, Jack Ging, Ted Hartley and Mitchell Ryan. They are a captivating group of duplicitous vermin and most of the reason the movie works.

High Plains Drifter sits comfortably in the company of the revisionist Westerns that came with the new politics and new social consciousness of the sixties - Altman's *McCabe and Mrs. Miller* and *Buffalo Bill and the Indians*, the *Man-Called-Horse* series, Walter Hill's *The Long Riders,* Sam Peckinpah's *The Wild Bunch,* and more. Tidyman's cynicism is so all-encompassing the movie seems unrepeatable without familiarity breeding contempt. Eastwood will be consistently drawn to downbeat stories. They will seldom be offered in such an airtight package.

The Eiger Sanction – 1975

Not only is *The Eiger Sanction* a racist, sexist and homophobic movie - it also bashes a disability - in this case, albinism. The story is crass and tasteless and, like the rape scene in *High Plains Drifter*, an early hint of why it becomes hard to see Eastwood's amorality as anything other than sordid sensationalism. The only way we could get Eastwood off the hook on a movie this bad is to suggest he was just a hired hand; he was given the script and commanded to shoot it; but by 1975, Eastwood was picking the movies he wanted to film. *The Eiger Sanction* begins a pattern in Eastwood's films: he sounds off racist, homosexual, misogynist dog whistles for laughs, and layers on violent histrionics for the amusement of his basest audience.

Vonetta McGee plays a stewardess named "Jemima." We learn her name during a dimwitted and condescending conversation on an airplane with Eastwood's Dr. Hemlock (he's some kind of professorial egghead not too clearly delineated). In an implausible manner common to Eastwood films, Jemima isn't offended and flirts with Hemlock. He will later bed her and refer to her as "Aunt Jemima."

Brenda Venus plays "George" (this may be one of the most stupidly named group of characters ever assembled in a film); George is an "American Indian." Hemlock lets her know he "wished Custer had won." She beds him anyway - attracted not by his racism, but because she is a spy setting him up to be murdered. Other of the film's sordid female roles are awarded to Heidi Bruhl and Candace Rialson.

Jack Cassidy is Miles Mellough, a gay nemesis who once betrayed Hemlock when they were partners in some kind of international spy organization. Mellough has a dog named "Faggot." At one point the genius Dr. Hemlock remarks on Mellough's homosexuality: "you have an incurable disease and are too afraid to kill yourself."

Thayer David is "Dragon." The head of the aforementioned organization - he's an albino who needs periodic blood transfusions to stay alive.

Eastwood's weakness for needless digression is on display from the first sequence of *The Eiger Sanction*. The movie starts in a college school room. Eastwood puts on a pair of glasses so we can accept him as a professor of art. His attempt to squeeze out the erudite phrases is laughable. Higher learning isn't the point. The blonde female in the front row of his class (Rialson) is spreading her legs provocatively and Hemlock leers at her in a repellent manner, unnoticed by the rest of his students. Soon the girl will be in Hemlock's office propositioning herself in an attempt to raise her grades. He slaps her ass and sends her away in gentlemanly fashion. We could call this pointless to the plot if Eastwood didn't consciously devise his plots to invoke perverted guffaws in the movie audience, which I'm sure materialized here and there throughout America.

The internationalism of *The Eiger Sanction* is lazily depicted. Dr. Hemlock is an ex-assassin. His ex-boss, the aforementioned Dragon, wants to pull him in for one last hit. In Zurich, an American courier has been murdered and the microfilm he was carrying containing the formula for a new germ has been stolen. Will Hemlock please go and terminate the two men responsible for the theft and murder? Hemlock doesn't want to, but he has been illegally obtaining black market art (Pissarro, Matisse, etc.) and Dragon threatens to turn him in to the IRS. Hemlock accepts the assignment.

The next thing we know, Hemlock is scaling up a building via a rain gutter, sneaking in a back window and dispatching with little consequence the first bad guy. Eastwood's direction makes the whole scene rather perplexing because you can't tell where the action is taking place - it seems to be the USA - are the Swiss bad guys in America now?

Anyway, Dragon tells Dr. Hemlock that the second bad guy has "a limp." The only other information: this bad guy will be on a climbing expedition up the infamous Eiger Mountain.   Since there are only three other people on the climb - a limp should be easily spotted on first meeting - but nobody limps. Dr. Hemlock will have to join the mountaineers to figure it out. Luckily his old friend, climbing instructor Ben Bowman (George Kennedy), will help with some quick mountain-climbing training.

The film takes a long time to get to the outdoor action and it is anti-climactic.   Supposedly shot on location in Switzerland, the mountain-climbing scenes are claustrophobic. There is little sense provided of landscape or weather, but Eastwood's ass keeps getting stuck on rocks. Hemlock goes up the mountain - and guess what? With the exception of Hemlock, the mountaineers all fall off and die, and there is no spy anywhere to be seen.

But wait, remember Hemlock's friend and climbing instructor Bowman - the one that Hemlock had been hanging around with for a number of days, even climbing a monument with him - well, suddenly for not much of a stated reason, Bowman is limping when Eastwood comes off the mountain. But that's okay - they remain friends because it seems the whole thing was a ruse - the microfilm that had been stolen was actually a "false" formula - and Dragon just wanted the thieves to be killed so it would add believability to the fact that Americans are nefarious or something.

So, what else can Hemlock do but hang around the pool at the mountain resort, drink booze and get ready to boff "Aunt Jemima" again. Mourning for the innocent dead skiers will take place elsewhere.

The Outlaw Josey Wales – 1976

In a reissue of *The Outlaw Josey Wales* on DVD, Clint Eastwood offers a personal introduction to the film. He cites the movie as the Western he is particularly proud of directing. He says the film is about "war and the effect it has on people." That certainly sounds better than "another Western revenge fantasy bereft of acting logic with yet another character-free, superhuman gunman hogging up the air in the story."

The plot opens in Civil War era Missouri with the overly-familiar sketch about a simple farmer named Josey Wales (Clint in yokel hat and overalls) plowing a tough field only to be startled by an attack on his farm by a group of "Red Legs" - Kansas militiamen known for looting, pillaging and murdering while they ostensibly fight for the Union against the Confederate army. The Red Legs abscond with Josey Wales' wife; his young son is burned alive in the family farmhouse. Wales had attempted to intervene but was knocked out and disfigured leaving a scar across his face that will come and go throughout the movie.

Wales wakes up to find a group of Confederate renegades under the command of Captain Fletcher (John Vernon) in pursuit of the Red Legs. Wales joins them and there is a clumsily filmed montage of the riders burning and hanging and looting in their own fashion with Eastwood statuesque among them. There will be no philosophical underpinning related to the scales of justice, no *Ox-Bow Incident* ruminations on the implications of taking justice into your own hands. The rules of war don't apply to either the Red Legs, the Union or Fletcher's Confederate band - they are mirrors of each other. Slavery is implicitly defended both by complete occlusion in the plot and the fact that these Confederate boys are for some reason the *good* bad guys while those attempting to free the slaves are the *bad* bad guys. The general mind-set seems left over from the source material - a novel written by ex-KKK leader Forest Carter and entitled *Josey Wales: The Rebel Outlaw*.

In order to set Wales' cutthroat barbarians in relief, Eastwood has to suggest the Union soldiers are slightly more barbaric. When the war ends, Union officers offer amnesty to Captain Fletcher and his murderous band. Fletcher leads his men to surrender but Wales refuses to go - he will never surrender until he gets the Red Legs that destroyed his family. Why he couldn't surrender and still kill them I'm not sure, but it's lucky he doesn't because Fletcher's confederates are betrayed and dispatched with a Union Gatling gun. The role Captain Fletcher played in this trap will remain confusing throughout the film. Josey Wales escapes but not before getting hold of a Gatling gun himself and taking out the whole regiment in easy Eastwoodian fashion. Thus, he becomes the "outlaw" Jose Wales pursued by the Red Legs, the Union, Captain Fletcher, and any number of bounty hunters and gunmen. From this moment forward the film becomes a schematic and fairly predictable move from point to point as Wales dispatches those who catch up to him or recognize him because sometimes the scar appears on his face and sometimes it doesn't.

Philip Kaufman (director of *The White Dawn*, *The Wanderers*, *The Right Stuff*, *Unbearable Lightness of Being*, *Rising Sun*) co-wrote the script, set up the pre-production and began directing the film but was fired by Eastwood. You can see the outline of Kaufman's own directorial obsessions in the film - the chaotic interplay of tribe against tribe - the Red Legs, Captain Fletcher's men, the multi-cultural and blood-thirsty Comancheros, the virgin-raping and violent Comanche, Indian-raping fur-trappers, the religious but hard-bitten new settlers, and various bounty hunters. Any thematic depth Kaufman might have pull of the film - democratic impulses breaking towards or from tribal dynamics, and the impenetrable and qu cultural wall that separates groups from groups an individual from the group - is well beyond Eastwood's taciturn preoccupations.

Eastwood hits his gunfighter marks in a numb colorful locales. As *Variety Magazine* put it: "ca production numbers [are] slotted every so often." The length of the film never finds an epic theme and the spec is empty of emotion. Even the revenge aspect gets los Wales is so intent on killing the Red Legs - why does he r further and further away from them? Why do the Red 1 have to find him in order for the final showdown to place?

Eastwood's introductory comments to the DVD suggest he interpreted the screenplay as the general softening of a man after the horrors of war, but that certainly isn't in the arc of his acting or the arc of his story-telling. The murderous back-story is too generic to frame Wales within any reality of psychological trauma or physical struggle (as compared to films from Budd Boetticher's *Decision at Sundown* to Alejandro Inarritu's *The Revenant*). Eastwood's acting style is too restricted to depict much more than what is suggested by the blank slate - mostly "manliness." Never registered is a repugnance toward violence, just a calm demeanor against all odds. Wales boasts the usual eyes-in-the-back-of-his-head ability to handle any challenge with preposterous dexterity - sometimes he's doing acrobatics on his horse that don't make sense from a physics standpoint, another time he's handing over his guns by the barrel only to flip them over and shoot the bad guys. It's the kind of stuff a ten-year-old carries around in his head as heroic acts. As Wales meets any number of people along his escape route - an old Indian, an Indian squaw, a group of settlers, a dog, a group of townspeople - everybody is fun-grumpy rather than war-weary.

For a film with the Civil War as the background, African-Americans are nowhere to be seen. But we do get a lot of Native Americans. These scenes keep hitting off-notes of condescension. Not so much in the way Lone Watie (Chief Dan George) and Little Moonlight (Geraldine Kearns) are used for comic effect, but in the overly-giddy spectacle of funny subservient Indians siding up with a Confederate murderer. Robert Ebert would be reminded of the old Western comic relief of sidekicks like Gabby Hayes, but how can the comic relief of Stepin Fetchit not be far behind?

Further out-of-left-field is Wales' penultimate meeting with Ten Bears (Will Sampson) and his group of Comanche killers. The Comanches have two of Wales' acquaintances buried up to their head in dirt. The tribe is ready to take out Wales and the settlers. Buried or not, little distress is registered on all sides by anybody but the Comanche. Wales confronts Ten Legs on horseback and suddenly the ex-farmer shows a vast knowledge of Comanche history and philosophical beliefs as he penetrates the deep recesses of their soul while chit-chatting about "life" and "death." Wales promises to carry the Comanche sign, always help them, their fight will be his fight - and the Comanche are fooled, the settlers are dug up out of the ground showing little injury and ready to celebrate, and all the white people go back to their homes where they live in peace - with only a short break for Wales to dispatch his remaining Red Leg nemesis Capt. Terrill (Bill McKinney) before a brief portentous chat with Captain Fletcher which makes absolutely no sense.

The Gauntlet - 1977

Ben Shockley (Eastwood) is a police detective assigned to bring a witness in a federal case back to Phoenix from a Las Vegas jail. His superior, Commissioner Blakelock (William Prince), assures him that he is delivering a non-witness in a nothing-case and not to worry. He tells Shockley that people have recommended him for the job because he always "gets the job done."

The witness is a prostitute named Gus Mally (Sandra Locke) privy to mob connections and sexual perversion relating to the Phoenix police force. Shockley retrieves Mally but has been set up and soon the mob and the Las Vegas police are trying to kill him and his witness. This involves narrow escapes and a gradual bonding between Shockley and Mally.

The usual escapades ensue. Shoot-em-ups, explosions and a car chased by a helicopter. Because the character definition is buried in the plot details, and not supported by Eastwood's actions or interactions, a bit of back-story comes way too late. At first you think Shockley is another Dirty Harry substitute (his resourcefulness in the face of violent provocations suggests "prowess"). It takes more than half the movie to realize Shockley's been picked for witness protection because he's considered incompetent, so a poignant scene arrives as a complete surprise. Shockley and Mally are stuck in the desert after escaping a shoot-out with the Las Vegas police that destroys Mally's home. Mally makes Shockley realize he's been picked to deliver her because he's an expendable "nobody" who nobody will miss and is considered too stupid to finish the mission. Watching this sink in (not on Eastwood's face, but somewhere within the blankness of expression that allows you to project) reminds you that there is no reason why a movie like this couldn't contain an original character, even given Eastwood's acting abilities.

In one uncomfortable scene, Shockley and Mally jump on a box car right into the hands of the remnants of a motorcycle gang. They beat Shockley up, tie him down and continue to beat him. Mally begins taking off her clothes to distract the thugs and they begin brutalizing her, but Shockley, much like the incredible Hulk, breaks his bindings and tosses the bullies off the train.

The worst scene of all is probably the following:

There is a long sequence when Shockley and Mally kidnap a highway patrolman and hi-jack his car. As the patrolman drives, Shockley is in the passenger seat holding a gun to the patrolman's head. Mally is in the middle of the back seat looking on. There is something distracting about Eastwood's performance here as he waves the gun about; the gun looks too heavy, like he can barely hold it up. The patrolman picks up on Mally being a prostitute and launches into a scatological, masturbatory diatribe. He asks Mally how many times a month she spreads her legs. He talks about her gash, and her deep wetness, and asks where she learned to give head. He mentions that he almost started a whorehouse once and he was going to advertise it as "finger-lickin' good." He keeps up the dirty talk until his face suggests he is reaching some sort of orgasmic climax. Eastwood seems frozen as to how he is supposed to be reacting as an actor - he just continues to wave the gun about. But here are the real overriding non-artistic concerns in this horrible scene:

Firstly: It's a *Tab Cola* commercial.

The whole time you're watching this horrid display a *Tab Cola* can is smashed into your consciousness right in front of the action on the patrol car dashboard and magnified in hierarchy so you can't miss it. And it's there for a long time - it doesn't rattle, or move, or fall no matter how fast the car goes.

Secondly: I will suggest something morally worse than the general ugliness of the language and the *Tab* commercial, and it goes back to Eastwood's awkwardness in maneuvering the gun within this three-person ensemble. The scene is first and foremost a GUN advertisement. The gun has to stay as relevant in the brand hierarchy as the *Tab Cola*. And the way it dips and bobs a bit may just be because it's heavy and Eastwood is having a hard time holding it up for this way too long adventure in advertising. What he is doing here as a gun salesman is no different from his *Smith and Wesson* ads in an earlier *Dirty Harry* film, or the *Magnum* commercial in *Magnum Force*. (*Unforgiven* will eventually feature the most gun advertisements - *Smith & Wesson*, *Schofield*, *Colt*, even a small *Philadelphia Derringer* will get a brief spotlight).

Commercials over, as Shockley and Mally get closer to Phoenix they are told the whole police force has lined the streets to the courthouse waiting for their return. It never occurs to them to make a few phone calls to the press or to their congressmen. Instead, Shockley hi-jacks a large bus filled with passengers, drives the vehicle to some kind of metal-works garage, and dumps the passengers. In a matter of minutes and with unbelievable flair, Shockley welds together and fashions an armored vehicle out of the bus (the bus passengers are still standing by like they had to wait to congratulate him before they can leave). Shockley and Mally use the armored bus to run the police "gauntlet." Thousands of bullets are shot at the bus but nobody ever hits a tire - and that's some kind of metaphor for Eastwood films in general.

Most critics were unkind, but Roger Ebert came through with a three-star review that embarrassed the category by claiming *The Gauntlet* was "classic Clint Eastwood: fast, furious and funny."

Any Which Way but Loose – 1978
(A Non-Digression Directed by James Fargo)

Every Which Way but Loose shows us how, at this point, even an Eastwood vehicle helmed by another director was expected to touch bases of misogyny and anti-liberalism. James Fargo had served as assistant director on several Eastwood films and was obviously familiar with the Eastwood template. There are at least 5 stupid fights in the film (there might be more, I admit I abandoned the film just before the ending).

Set in a San Fernando Valley that seems populated by Louisiana hillbillies, Eastwood plays Philo Beddoe - a "truck driver" living in a trailer-parkish group of homes with his "Ma" (Ruth Gordon cussing up a storm) and his pet orangutan "Clyde." The movie adds "morphydite" to Eastwood's list of insults and animal exploitation to his oeuvre.

Take this sequence: Philo is sporting a cowboy hat in a club where a country band featuring Mel Tillis is playing. He spots a couple of young women and says to his friend Orville (Geoffrey Lewis) "I'll take the one on the left." He also adds mysteriously - "she's eating clam chowder." He approaches one of the women and makes some dumb asides. She rebuffs him. He continues to flirt. Irritated, she says her name is Carol, she goes to USC and is writing a sociological paper on the country-western "mentality." (Eastwood is setting her up. It's an Eastwoodian idea of the "too-smart" girl.) When Carol gets up to go to the bathroom Philo calls to Orville and Orville hands Philo a nasty dental insert. He slips it into Carol's soup (they must do this all the time ha, ha, ha - that's a lot of dental inserts to have to carry around ha, ha, ha; she deserves it because she's a woman with aspirations and she doesn't like Philo ha, ha, ha). The woman returns and he asks her what she's found out about the country-western mentality. She replies, "if the lyrics of this song are any indication, it's somewhere between moron and dull-normal." He tells her to enjoy her clam chowder. She discovers the teeth and screams.

Later, Philo and Orville fall for a couple of very, very, loose women. Philo is smitten by the musical talents of Lynn Halsey-Taylor (Sandra Locke playing a con-artist / country-western singer). Greasy Orville unconvincingly cajoles Echo, a vendor at a farmer's market (a sadly-cast though very lively Beverly D'Angelo) to run away with him - I guess just because somebody asks her to.

After a sexual dalliance, Lynn the singer rips off Philo's cash and flees town. Philo takes Orville, Echo and Clyde the orangutan and they head out in pursuit of Lynn, leaving Ma at home fighting off eviction notices. Along the way a swastika-sporting motorcycle gang called The Spiders, looking like they escaped from the sixties *Muscle Beach Party* movies, take umbrage to Philo and start trying to kill him.

Clyde, the orangutan, is a horrid sight to watch. Every time his individual tricks / scenes end, his face slackens, his eyes lurch about and you can almost see him reaching for his reward. Some actors will do anything for recompense. In Clyde's case, it appears to be peanuts and beer.

Every Which Way but Loose would become one of the biggest money-makers of the year and would spawn the sequel *Any Which Way You Can.*

Honkytonk Man - 1982

It's depression-era Oklahoma. Drunk and nearly catatonic at the wheel of a convertible during a calamitous dust storm, Red Stovall (Clint Eastwood) careens into his brother-in-law's farmyard after a long trip. The storm will leave the farm destroyed. His sister (Verna Bloom) and her husband (Matt Clark) talk about leaving for California. Red is on the way to Nashville though; he's been given an opportunity to perform at the Grand Ole Opry. Red's nephew, fourteen-year-old Whit (played by Eastwood's son Kyle), is smitten with his uncle. When Red invites him to go along, Whit jumps at the chance to leave farm life behind. His parents seem oddly happy to release him into the care of a drunkard. Grandpa (John McIntire) wants to go to Nashville too - back to the South where he was raised. Another son and a daughter float around in these early scenes, but they function almost as neglected extras.

Verna Bloom with her raw sunburn and Matt Clark with his stressed intensity certainly look the part, but any pretense that this is a drama about the Depression a la *Bound for Glory*, *Bonnie and Clyde*, or *Grapes of Wrath* is lost in a quick minute.

Similarly, any idea that this is a movie about country-western music and a country-western music man is abandoned as quickly as Eastwood's Okie accent. Given the evidence here, Eastwood is such a mediocre singer and musician it's no wonder his screen time avoids any insights into the folk-art quest or country music craft. Eastwood never shows us the talent in Red that everybody is supposedly talking about.

What *Honkytonk Man* ends up being is part episodic road movie and part coming-of-age tale. Not only is Red an alcoholic riddled with tuberculosis, he is also a chicken thief, a bar robber, and likes brothels. Underwritten escapades unwind as Red approaches Nashville. We get to watch Red introduce Whit to a brothel. Red participates in a botched robbery. Whit breaks Red out of jail. Everything is pushed along in a lighthearted, inconsequential manner.

Whit follows Red with a certain open-mouthed wonder that is never humanly centered. I'm not sure there is a good scene in the film though Barry Corbin and Tracey Walter provide some fleeting true grit in a few moments of screen time as low-life rapscallions. Corbin plays Arnspriger; he owes Red money. To pay Red off, Arnspriger sets up a robbery. The robbery will be fake, the bar woman is in on it, "just tell her Arnspriger sent you." Carrying a shotgun into the bar and pointing it at the female bartender, Red tells those present "Arnspriger sent me" and he quite authentically scares the poor woman almost to death, and a long bout of screaming ensues. It's the kind of violence Eastwood loves playing for laughs and it's beyond redemption - this honky-tonk man is as morally oblivious as the director to the unexplored subtexts of trauma that run rampant throughout the film.

Red's last chance at country-western fame and fortune ends with a ridiculously played sequence in Nashville. Red's TB cough destroys his Grand Ole Opry audition, yet for some reason a couple of record people are impressed. They invite the near-dead wheezer to a recording session and try to coax out the last remnants of his handful of mediocre songs. Again, the TB cough gets him, and Marty Robbins leans in to finish the movie's title song. After Red dies, Whit and a female companion are walking down the street on their way to California. A teenage couple drive by with their car radio blasting Red's "Honkytonk Man."

Racist Watch: The scene where Grandpa muses eloquently on how much fun it was to steal land from the Cherokee territory. Love those All-American Grandpas.

Sudden Impact - 1983

This entry in the *Dirty Harry* series was the only one directed by Eastwood. Every sequel that followed Donald Siegel's original classic was filled with clichés and *Sudden Impact* is no different. For instance, this scene: Harry is illegally target practicing in a Bay-Area forest (take that you liberal redwoods and you mealy-mouthed park rangers). Unbeknownst to Harry, an African-American in a huge car is sneaking up "quietly" into the thicket a short distance away. He gets out of the car and slides a rifle out of his car window. He "carefully" sneaks up behind Harry (I say "carefully" and "quietly" because he makes so much noise you expect Harry with his superhuman ears to turn around and shoot him dead). The man raises his rifle. Harry wheels around in surprise: but we, the audience, have already figured this out - this particular African-American will be Harry's "black movie friend" and his name is Horace (Albert Popwell). Horace joins the various African-American, Hispanic-American or female partners who make appearances in Eastwood films only to be ridiculed before being grudgingly accepted and/or quickly dispatched without establishing much of a presence. Horace is in maybe two additional scenes: one in which he tells Harry what a great cop he is (African-American affirmation); another in which Horace is murdered by the bad guys.

As with the rest of the *Dirty Harry* series, *Sudden Impact* uses San Francisco locations. The film opens with wondrously beautiful views of the San Francisco skyline. This isn't a foggy San Francisco film noir - everything happens in bright and sunny locales. Lalo Schifrin's score offers a buoyant paean to the city. The overcast ambiance that Don Siegel supplied to *Dirty Harry* (with Bruce Surtees on board) or the grittier atmosphere Peter Yates gave to *Bullit* is nowhere to be seen. This is a Bruce Surtees tourism postcard.

The San Francisco landscape exudes neither sordidness or despair yet everywhere old Harry goes somebody is robbing a bank, or throwing a Molotov cocktail into his car window, or trying to shoot him into pieces with a machine gun. He can't even go into a café to get a cup of coffee without walking into a gang-style robbery. The labored histrionics of these crimes are particularly laughable if you happen to be a San Francisco native - which I am. Long, loud gunfights outside the Embarcadero Plaza with not a single person anywhere in sight; long, loud car chases around the Wharf without a single car in sight (it's definitely not tourist season). The restaurant robbery is particularly foolish: a black gang attempts a robbery in broad daylight in a brightly lit café with huge, cleanly washed windows that clearly show all activity to the cars, bicycles and pedestrians passing close by on the sidewalk and street. It is here that Harry will make the preposterously stupid "Make My Day" speech so splendidly parodied a few years later by Robert Townsend in *Hollywood Shuffle*, in which Townsend suggested any brother would have shot Harry somewhere during the long wheezy pauses between "Make" and "My" and "Day."

In one scene, Harry crashes a fancy party, approaches a table, and coaxes an old mobster into a heart attack. In real life these actions might have ended up with a charge of manslaughter and probably a lawsuit. No wonder all of Harry's superiors yell at him in unnaturally loud voices and decide to push him out of town.

More carelessly plotted episodic diversions keep the film treading water until the vanishing plot line reemerges. If all of the needless padding had been excised by a conscientious editor or a frugal producer the subsequent 50-minute film might have been a little better.

So, let's find those threads. It is early dawn in San Francisco at a well-known spot where the Golden Gate Bridge is easily seen along the SF Bay shoreline. A car is parked close to the edge of the high cliff. Inside the car a couple are in a fully-clothed embrace. The woman "stealthily" reaches into her handbag and pulls out a revolver and puts a bullet into the man's crotch, and then gives him one in the head. She climbs out of the car and walks over to the cliff's edge with her gun at her side and stares down at the water. Again, if you are a San Francisco resident you wonder where everybody went: all the early morning joggers, the dog walkers, the spry tourists, the shore hikers, and the homeless people. You may also be somewhat perplexed as to how the woman is going to get home since she doesn't seem to have brought a car, the likelihood of getting a taxi this far out would be time-consuming, and the trek to the nearest commuter train would be rather risky considering the circumstances.

The woman in question is Jennifer Spencer (Sandra Locke). Jennifer's character points don't really need to be elaborated other than to say this is a woman-and-her-sister-were-raped / traumatized scenario, and this blonde is out to get revenge on the men who did her and her sister wrong. *Sudden Impact* is not a mystery, or a procedural crime drama, nor does it have true crime ambiance like the original *Dirty Harry*.

When Harry is sent to the crime scene to investigate the murder - given all his talk about "justice" and "law and order" - you would expect him to be a stickler for detail; instead, he stares dumbly at the water and takes the most cursory glance at the car where the murder took place. It's bizarre - and suggests Harry can only react when contrived violent scenarios are thrown at him, but for anything that requires regular detective work, he's too lazy. (A more obvious explanation is that Eastwood has wasted so much time on melodramatic action that crime scene exploration is not available in the film's budget).

In a flashback we learn that Jennifer and her sister were raped at a carnival ground in San Paulo, California by a group of hooligans. The assault is directed so badly it looks like the girls are being ravaged in plain sight of a fully-loaded Ferris wheel. Jennifer goes to visit her sister at some kind of convalescent center. The doctor tells Jennifer her sister is unresponsive to treatment. Her sister is in a wheelchair and seems comatose, though her eyes are open. Jennifer informs her sister that she has killed one of the men responsible. And here's the problem: the audience sees that her sister suddenly has tears streaming down her face - surely this is some kind of medical breakthrough, right? But Jennifer is behind her and doesn't see this. Jennifer turns and leaves. What does this all mean? We never find out.

Anyway, after the San Francisco killing, Jennifer heads to San Paulo at the same time every person who works with Harry wants him to go away somewhere so he doesn't attract every multi-cultural criminal in the Bay Area to wherever he happens to be walking. His superiors tell him he's being given the "shoreline murder case" and that the victim in the car was from San Paulo so go there and follow the leads. Harry doesn't want to leave; he loves San Francisco too much, I guess. But he heads up there and rather easily meets Jennifer while jogging (just by coincidence); he stops an armed robbery (just by coincidence); and he runs into the nest of rapists at a local bar (this also seems somewhat by coincidence although some kind of information has arrived from somewhere).

A word about this armed robbery just mentioned: In order to pursue the thief who has fled on a motorcycle, Harry steals a bus carrying a bunch of geriatric patients (a repeat from *The Gauntlet*). This group of old people think the chase is a lot of fun; the endangering lives, and suing the cops will not be a consideration.

Jennifer begins offing the gang one by one. A few white people are involved including the gang's abusive leader Ray (Audrie Neenan) who is referred to as "the dyke." Neenan's gleeful sadism is about the only compelling thing in this movie, the rest of the gang act like the three stooges.

Before Harry realizes Jennifer is the murderer, he sleeps with her and kind of likes her. They have a discussion about law and revenge and Harry finds a soul mate. The duo's argument in favor of vigilantism is also a pretty strong argument for moral depravity. Perhaps the championing of moral depravity has been Eastwood's goal all along. On the other hand, Eastwood's characters generally don't display any real grievances worth considering on any level - right wing or left wing. By this point Harry isn't righteous - he's just perpetually grumpy and befuddled. Harry ends up liking Jennifer so much that when he finds out Jennifer is the killer, he doesn't let her take the fall.

As a byword, I have to mention the dog in the film. When Harry first arrives at his hotel in San Paulo, he enters the darkness of his rented room and stumbles over something. He turns on the light, looks around and there is this decrepit looking bulldog sort of hobbling around on the floor as if he's having a hard time getting up. Is he hurt? Seems like it. Harry finds out he's a joke present from his black friend Horace who hasn't died yet. Harry names the dog Meathead. Later, returning to his hotel room with Meathead in tow, the dog starts sniffing around the hotel room door right next to Harry's. Harry gets suspicious and grabs a gun at the precise moment a gunman bursts from the room intent on killing him. Harry shoots him dead and thanks Meathead. Later, Horace goes to Harry's room, but killers are waiting to kill Harry. They dispatch Horace and leave. Harry returns and sees Horace dead on the floor. Then he sees Meathead wobbling around the floor. Is Meathead hurt too? Seems like it. In a film like this – who knows?

Sudden Impact is another Eastwood vehicle meant to appeal to yahoos. There is enough gun fetish going on to keep safe Eastwood's "A" rating with the NRA. Right wing fantasies of conspiratorial liberal bureaucracy getting in the way of Wild West retribution had become a staple of Eastwood's films but it's always more implied than argued. When Pauline Kael called Don Siegel's *Dirty Harry* archetypal "fascist medievalism" with a "fairy-tale appeal" she was stating what was clearly effective about that film as propaganda. What Siegel did was mastered. What Eastwood does is just a stupid mess.

By 1983, Eastwood's coyness on the subject was already irritating. He would claim he wasn't telling people to "go out and buy a *Glock* and shoot people" (even when giving interviews Eastwood can't stop selling guns). He would stress that he had "made an anti-capital punishment movie called "Hang 'Em High" and nobody gave him credit for that (but he didn't "make" that film - it was directed by Ted Post and written by Leonard Freeman). Eastwood never delves deep enough into his right-wing predilections for them to mean anything more than what is suggested on the surface. And what is on the surface? Well, there is a reason why the brutish Rodrigo Duterte, the current President of the Philippines known for his drug enforcement death squads, has been referred to as Duterte Harry.

Pale Rider - 1985

Imagine a wide-open grassy space backed by beautiful snow-peaked mountains. In the distance: the sound of horse hooves. Soon: a fast-traveling group of horsemen can be discerned on the horizon. Cut closer: louder hooves, horses moving fast leaving dust behind them. Cut to a small stream where miners are stooped over their work, panning for gold. Cut to the horses: now we see the men, and they are armed. Cut to the miners. Cut to the horses. Cut to the miners. Cut to the horses. Cut to the miners - looking up - they think they hear something in the distance. Cut to the horses. Cut to the miners. Cut to the horses. Cut to the miners. It's a Mel Brooks parody.

Finally, the gang arrives to wreck mayhem in that time-weathered way that has launched many a bad Western. Tents are torn down, sluices are ruined, cattle shot, while the miners run stupidly about amongst the horses in an affectation of chaos. And then the gang is gone - hooves receding in the distance.

David Mamet has suggested movies would be better if the first ten minutes were excised? But where would you start with a film this bad?

Certainly not with the scene a few minutes later. Fourteen-year-old Megan Wheeler (Sydney Penny) has buried a pet dog that was shot during the raid. She recites the Lord's Prayer. As she prays for "a miracle" images of a mysterious rider appear super-imposed over her prayers. This will be

Preacher (Eastwood); where he comes from, we don't know (we are informed later his horse is called "Death").

The next day, one of the miners, Hull Barret (Michael Moriarty), who has been sheltering Megan's mother, Sarah Wheeler (Carrie Snodgrass), after her husband has deserted her, decides to go into town to get supplies against the warnings of the other miners. When Hull arrives, the corrupt businessman Coy LaHood (Richard Dysart) sends his men to confront him. They begin beating Hull mercilessly with axe handles. Enter Preacher, who pulls his own axe handle and renders the gang unconscious in a matter of a minute. It's another example of the Superman syndrome that makes these films easily dismissible. Nothing is at stake. Not only is Preacher not hurt, but Hull shows no discernable damage either.

Preacher offers nuggets of insight: i.e., when Hull tells him about his love for Sarah and her unshakeable reticence, Preacher says, "If you're waitin' for a woman to make up her mind, you'll be waitin' for a long time."

Shout out to Richard Kiel whom you might recall as the giant outlaw in *Butch Cassidy and the Sundance Kid* who gets his balls kicked in by Paul Newman. Here Kiel plays Club, who gets his balls smashed with a sledge hammer by Preacher. Kiel looks like he can hardly walk over the stony ground. Any menace he might once have shown had been lost with age.

LaHood tries to buy off Preacher, but it doesn't work. Lahood tells him he's going to bring in Marshall Stockburn (John Russell) and his hired henchmen to kill the miners. Preacher suggests that LaHood offer the miners 1000 dollars a head to leave their claims and LaHood accepts the idea. Preacher knows that Stockburn's gang are deadly because he's really not a Preacher but a gunfighter who has followed Stockburn from perhaps beyond the grave to exact revenge for putting 6 bullet holes through his chest.

When the miners decline the offer, LaHood calls in Marshall Stockburn and LaHood pontificates about the dangerous "faith" that the Preacher has brought to the miners as if this film is some kind of theological tome.

There is a creepy exchange with the young girl Megan, who has fallen in love with Preacher rather abstractly. It is night time and they are alone in the woods. She tells him she will be fifteen soon and begs him to show her how to make love. He declines and she argues it must be because Preacher likes her mother. She's seen Preacher "making eyes" at Sarah, but it seems pretty psycho on Megan's part because the story has provided no evidence that Preacher has an inordinate interest in her mother.

Another even creepier scene. After mother Sarah has professed her love for the miner Hull, Sarah goes to tell Preacher they are all leaving. Rather surprisingly she professes her love for Preacher, but tells him it will remain unconsummated. She kisses him saying "this is just so I won't be wondering about it for the next ten years." That's sort of okay, but when she opens the door to leave, from the hills in the background somebody is calling Preacher's name in spooky echoes. Maybe that's supposed to be the Marshall taunting him, I'm not sure. Preacher tells Sarah to close the door. She closes the door and walks back to him provocatively. It is assumed they will have intercourse, probably without protection. It's hard to say where this is all coming from and why Eastwood feels it necessary to piss on the womanhood aspects so thoroughly. Perhaps he is just fulfilling his one-sex-scene-per-movie obligation. Whatever bearing this all has on the more sanctimonious aspects of the script is hard to decipher. Bruce Surtees shot these indoor scenes so darkly, perhaps Preacher had been making eyes at Sarah but it was too dark for the audience to see. (The artsy lighting, which suggests an attempt at natural lighting, operates much like the montage in the opening scenes - technique hiding emptiness.)

The miners once again have their camp wrecked. One of the miners has discovered a big vein of gold. He is murdered by the Marshall's gang, so Hull and Preacher take some dynamite and destroy LaHood's expensive mining site. Preacher ditches Hull and rides off on his own to confront Stockburn's gang. Preacher offs the gang by hiding in various locations around the town and picking them off in fairly lackluster fashion. He confronts Marshall Stockburn in the street. They do the gunfight thing and Preacher puts 6 bullet holes in Stockburn's chest. From a nearby window LaHood sees Stockburn go down and he attempts to shoot Preacher with a rifle, but Hull, who has wandered in, shoots and kills LaHood.

Preacher rides off into the mountains, Megan yelling his name into the hills. He is returning to that faraway land of bad movie ideas.

Heartbreak Ridge - 1986

Fifteen years into his directing career Eastwood delivered a macho fantasy version of the USA/Ronald Reagan/Marine invasion of the island of Granada which took place on October 25, 1983. Ostensibly serious, the film carries all the gravity of an aged *McHale's Navy* episode. Plots twists are telegraphed, comedic moments are heavy handed, romantic interaction is formulated. The big finale - the assault on Granada - looks like it was filmed in Burbank. The action throughout is half-hearted and horribly edited. The jokes at the expense of "faggots" and women are intended for Eastwood's easiest audience - you don't want to lose the base - sometimes the base is all you have. Even the Army held their noses on viewing this film, refusing sponsorship tie-ins and other support which Eastwood loudly whined about. Not only does the movie shame the Marines, but the abusive language probably comes from Eastwood's lazy army days way back in the fifties. Most likely the Army viewed the scenes where Eastwood humorously strafes his platoon with machine gun fire as rightfully horrific given on-going problems with fragging (the intentional killing of fellow soldiers, mostly officers) and ongoing problems with friendly fire incidents - like those on USA Army bases that are currently making the news as I write. The director was hopelessly out of touch on all counts.

Eastwood is Tom Highway - a highly decorated Marine who has served in Korea and Vietnam, but is currently adrift - we meet him in jail after a drunken revelry that included urinating on a police vehicle. In his jail cell he brags about past exploits with women with various diseases. As you might expect, the meanest, overly-muscled cell-mate challenges Highway's stories and demeans his military service. Highway knocks him out in a predictable Eastwood manner (not only will a similar scene play itself out later on in the Marine barracks, but another similar scene comes close to being repeated in a bar).

Highway's superior officers have no use for him. He's a relic of the "old army." They also suggest he is a renegade though we get no examples of serious rebellion - just drunkenness and snarky remarks. Somebody up there takes pity on Highway and grants his wish to return "back home to Recon" - and we are quickly thrust into that familiar plot involving the hardened veteran who has to whip a crew of motley newbies into shape. The assignment brings him back to the locale of his ex-wife Aggie (Marsha Mason) whom he still finds attractive.

The film is riddled with Eastwood's lack of directorial attention and is practically a primer on how not to make a movie:

- Check out the scene where Mario Van Peebles in a silly overplayed role as a rapping rock star / Marine recruit named Stitch is on a crowded bus with Highway. He sings at the top of his lungs, curses, makes obnoxious jokes but the extras on the bus have obviously been told not to show any reaction.

- Check out the scene where Stitch jumps up on stage and sings loud rock and roll to a Marine bar crowd - but he never has a microphone. This is extremely loud music but when Highway's ex-wife comes over to talk to him - the band suddenly can't be heard and Clint exchanges pleasantries with her in his usual strangled whispers.

- Check out the lascivious waitress in the café that Stitch and Highway visit during a bus break - the waitress sees Highway's war medals and is ready to jump into the bathroom for some quick sex. Although the embarrassment of watching sex in the bathroom is thankfully avoided, when Highway scurries to catch the bus, the waitress runs outside and sends him off with a creepy open-mouthed tongue-protruding lick of her lips.

The recruits are sold as idiots so thoroughly that it stamps them for the whole movie as jerks, screw-ups, lazy slobs even as they are supposed to be learning discipline, manhood and teamwork under Highway's stern gaze. There is a muscle-bound guy named Swede who doesn't say much. A Hispanic of some sort goes AWOL because he has a wife and kid to feed and has to take a second job because the Marines don't pay enough. There are several other recruits running about who drop a line here and there but it's hard keeping track. Peebles gets the most air-time and the most embarrassing lines - at one point, he and the rest of his buddies act out ad-libbing a rap song about Highway. The scene is so stupid it probably made African-American kids stomach-sick if for some unknown reason they accidentally wandered into a theater showing *Heartbreak Ridge*. Highway refers to his men as "queer-bait" and even manages an anti-ecology joke of sorts. At one point the marching recruits sound off to a song about "pussy" as they march past an enlisted woman recruit.

Sgt. Highway's nemesis in *Heartbreak Ridge* is Major Powers (Everett McGill). Powers is a graduate officer who has never seen battle, goes "by the book" and doesn't like Highway's recklessness (I was on his side). Highway has been working his recruits "hard." Powers sets up a training exercise between his unit and Highway's - whichever unit arrives first at a designated target will win 72 hours leave.

The mission ends in a draw - sort of negating the whole idea of Highway's competence in comparison to Powers'. The resolution will be a fight between the two units in a big muddy puddle of water. The resulting bare-backed slog-fest looks like a bunch of porn actors posing for a Tom Bianchi photo shoot. Finally, Powers and Highway duke it out with predictable results. What should be a penultimate scene of expanding manhood becomes withering nonsense.

Somehow these losers are thrust into war. The audience may not feel the transition. We get some of the silliest over-the-top military music for scenes of ships in transit. Our heroes will end up jumping out of a helicopter into the ocean, where they will swim to shore and assault, on their hands and knees, the beaches of California. Vince Canby in his positive review in the *New York Times* wrote: "It requires a certain crazy vision to transform the American invasion of Grenada into the equivalent of Iwo Jima." Actually, it required total avoidance of the actual event and complete cinematic ignorance - this is not vision, it is blindness.

It's a disgusting portrayal of battle with no back-story on what the hell is going on. The soldiers fight a few fellows going down a road. Even though they've been shooting those assault rifles and exploding grenades, when they burst into the hospital where American "hostages" are being held, a woman comes running naked out of a shower for a blast of unwarranted titillation just moments after our guys have left a few dead bodies lying in the dirt. The hostages appear to be movie extras and they cheer the "Marines" in none-too-convincing Hollywood extra fashion. Then the recruits continue on up the hill where they fight another couple of guys and capture the summit. Sgt. Highway has been successful - he promised to make his recruits "life takers" - and he did. Oh yeah, one of the Marines gets killed. One of the Marines I didn't quite recognize says, "Yo, guys - Profile is dead." Then the war is over.

Wives, families, marching bands welcome our heroes back home. Highway's Aggie is there waiting - just in time for the happy ending. But you can imagine the relationship will never work out - Highway is still a flagrant American asshole with no redeeming social values.

Behind the scenes, movement was afoot to get Eastwood nominated for an *Academy Award*.

****

Roger Ebert offered a positive view of *Heartbreak Ridge* and at this point you have to question the vague passing grades he gave to the worst of Eastwood's films. The superlatives reviewer, in whose ranks I would place Ebert, when courting sycophancy often strain for things to write about instead of just coming out and saying the obvious. If anything explains the general mediocrity of *Heatbreak Ridge* and Eastwood's efforts in general, it's that he's not very good at directing genre pictures. Ebert gave excuses for Eastwood deficiencies. He claimed Eastwood "caresses the material as if he didn't know B movies have gone out of style."

To equate *Heartbreak Ridge* to B movies on Ebert's abstract level is wrongheaded for several reasons. *Heartbreak Ridge* cost 15 million dollars to make, was well-advertised and widely screened across America. It simply doesn't qualify as a B movie. I would understand what he meant about the "caressing of B-movie material" if he was referring to blockbusters like *Raiders of the Lost Ark* or *Star Wars* which cost multi-millions and had their heads stuck in the past. Modern Hollywood B-movie material and huge budget material are often the same thing - badly executed or impersonal genre films heavily funded. If you actually want to look at how some small company, lower budget films compared - the actual independent or quasi-independent movies at the time, I'd suggest the imaginative story-telling of films like Oliver Stone's *Salvador*. Or the way the horror films of David Cronenberg elevate what used to be B movie subject matter into prime cinematic territory - *Videodrome*, *The Dead Zone* or *The Fly*, for example. David Lynch's *Blue Velvet* was shot for 6 million and it's a beautifully original film. Spike Lee was able to scrape together 175,000 dollars for the ground-breaking *She's Gotta Have It*. Even less for John Sayles' *Lianna* and *Baby It's You*. Ditto Jim Jarmusch's *Down by Law*. All of these stories are more original, better shot, better acted. Up on the more expensive scale, Michael Mann and William Friedkin had taken material from the same reservoir as Eastwood and served up much more compelling pictures. And compare *Heartbreak Ridge* to a war movie with a similar budget as Eastwood's that came out the same year, namely *Platoon* - and think about what that film has to say about war, violence, drugs, good, evil, and macho manliness vs. stoner empathy vs. intellectual scruples. Ebert is throwing up a smokescreen, he isn't looking at what's before his eyes.

Eastwood's movies trend towards something inferior to great old-style B movie-making. They are happy to be the most reductive of programmed star vehicles. They forego a huge and very important amount of screen time in order to regurgitate recurring crowd-pleasing patterns - fist fights, car chases, bad comedy, dated masculine stances, perfunctory sex scenes with women the protagonists hardly like, anti-authoritarian bullshit, bank robberies and gunfights. If you are looking for originality, quirkiness, subversion – you won't find it anywhere.

Trying to shove Eastwood into the ranks of the great B-movie directors doesn't acknowledge what great story-tellers, craftsmen, acting-directors, and money handlers they actually were - they got a whole lot for very little. Eastwood pales by comparison although he runs an old-style movie production company with a stock of company technicians and gets fairly big budgets. Eastwood movies often seem failures of pre-production - with the acceptance of the final script. When reading about the old pre-production process of Sam Fuller, Nicholas Ray, Donald Siegel, Robert Aldrich and others, one of the most recurring lines you run across is: "but they weren't happy with script." These directors / producers had to oversee writers who ironed out the clichés, strengthened the characters, tightened up the stories, and found a way to charge up emotional content that might match the action in a free-flowing cinematic manner. The best of the B movie directors were masters of quick headed form and fusion. If Donald Siegel films remain more varied, more emotionally grounded, more entertaining and more exciting than Eastwood's directing efforts - it's because the things Siegel left out are the things Eastwood kept putting in over and over and over again. Put another way, a script that Siegel wouldn't accept, is a script Eastwood would accept. In some ways, it's merely a matter of taste.

White Hunter, Black Heart - 1990

White Hunter, Black Heart is based on Peter Viertel's novel of the same name - a fictitious account of the writer's time spent with movie director John Huston in 1951 during the filming of *The African Queen*. According to this movie, once on location Huston (referred to here as John Wilson) wasn't in the mood to shoot the film. He was distracted by hopes of shooting an elephant in the African bush. Producers panicked; the actors sat around and drank.

Eastwood, with ever-present cigar, gives a quickly-tedious impression of Huston's dark and drooping speech patterns. He takes a leap he's never taken before - verbosity - and he fails miserably.

This version of Huston is repellent. Opening scenes introducing Huston's macho nature show him in hunting garb riding a horse around an English countryside. Afterwards Huston argues with his British producers about filming in Africa - they would prefer he stay closer to home, but in a demeaning manner he insists on location shooting. Eastwood does nearly the impossible here - he makes Huston's combative nature so abrasively rude you side with the money men.

Peter Viertel, the author of the novel, is named Pete Verrill for the film and is played by Jeff Fahey. There are quasi-philosophical discussions between writer and director about Hemingway, Flaubert and Melville which labor to establish an intellectual basis for all the macho mystique. The film's tone is off: it could have been played as the funny bullshit of an old self-deluded codger; or a serious reflection on dehumanizing obsession; but Eastwood isn't good at either comedy or obsession. There are two scenes with what I'll describe as stupid Eastwoodian "screwable" female stereotypes - one in England and one in Africa. The first is a woman who has a script idea she wants to sell to the director and he encourages her bad ideas in order to get her into bed - this is played with snickers and guffaws. When director and author land in Africa, they are introduced to their camp host and his wife - you want to yell at the screen and tell the wife to flee before the lechery asserts itself.

Most of the Huston-based dialogue is opaque gibberish destroyed by Eastwood's delivery. Any idea of a unique artist in a mental crisis is jettisoned in favor of Eastwood's slavish sense of reverence for the director's fictionalized creepy behavior.

In Africa there is bonding with Jews and the local natives. Every white person that lives in Africa seems racist so Wilson is there to show people the right way to treat their brothers. The director befriends a local African tribesman / hunter. The hunting scenes are detestable, poor leftover beasts of the fading world looking almost meek and mild as the hunters get ready to kill them. The climax is botched with some bad editing: Wilson finds the elephant beast he has been looking for, aims carefully, but has an unexplained crisis of conscience and doesn't shoot. As everybody gets ready to end the hunt, the elephant's baby runs into view and the big beast gets excited and charges the hunters. Wilson's African guide gets speared by the elephant's tusks and dies. This sequence is so rushed you hardly take it in.

The chastened director heads back to the film set. The natives are told their beloved tribesman is dead; they begin beating on their drums. "What's that say?" Wilson asks, referring to the drums. "What it always says," is the reply "White hunter, black heart." Wilson sits down in his director's chair and calls, "Action."

The Rookie – 1990

The Rookie is a uneasy entertainment just based on the large number of innocent people killed and injured directly related to the illegal actions perpetuated by the police officers involved in the sloppy storyline. In the first sequence, we meet Nick Pulovski (Eastwood) and his African-American partner Powell (Hal Williams) in pursuit of a gang of car thieves. Strom (Raul Julia who is puzzlingly noted as being "German" – though he and his crew are mostly Latino) is a murderous chop-shop kingpin. The gang has almost loaded up a big tractor trailer with stolen vehicles when Nick and Powell (they don't call for back-up) confront them. Nick holds two of the thieves at gunpoint while Powell goes up front to check the truck's cab. He opens the door and looks inside, but it's empty. He turns and shouts toward the back to Nick "There's nobody up here." But the truck door slowly closes behind him revealing Strom who shoots and kills Powell (a very short paycheck for Williams).

A shoot-out ensues and the crooks make their escape in the big rig. Nick pursues them down the freeway at high speeds. Multiple car crashes, flipped vehicles and general mayhem is the result; yet the culprits get away. A safe guess is the real-life destruction would have amounted to a few hundred thousand dollars in vehicle damages, plus broken necks, death, dismemberment – who knows – who has time to care? You expect Nick to show up back at headquarters and get the usual haranguing by his superiors even if this isn't a *Dirty Harry* film. Surprisingly, not a single word is mentioned about the mass destruction. Nick's superiors seem to like him although this scenario differs very little from all the other roles where Eastwood's character puts members of the community in unwarranted danger.

Added to this is a strange moment that comes later when Nick's new partner David Ackerman ("the rookie" of the title played by Charlie Sheen) asks him why he is intent on pursuing these particular car thieves. Nick rather unemotionally mentions his dead "partner," but this is quickly abandoned in favor of an unconvincing attempt at a back-story. Nick confesses that he had been a small-time racecar driver and a small-time cop. This is the first time a kingpin like Strom has fallen into his hands and he wants a big score. What might in past films have been revenge over a dead partner or loved one here shifts to pure hubris.

The Rookie is another superhero cop film. At one point, Sheen's David walks into a dark bar filled with strong Latino males, blows an alcohol-based fire into the bartender's face, beats up half the clientele and sends them running. Then he kills their attack dogs and burns the bar down.

Action is all and macho fantasy is the prevailing theme. There is the usual veteran cop / rookie cop banter. Two strands of back-story are given to the rookie. David was at least partially responsible for the death of his young brother when his brother fell while jumping across city roofs. This scrap of info is alluded to a few times but it's hard to see any psychological weight on David. The second bit of back-story reveals David as the black sheep in his very, very rich family – he's become a cop against the wishes of his parents (played by Tom Skerritt and Donna Mitchell). Little convincing drama results, but later in the film when Nick is kidnapped and held for ransom by Strom, David is able to get a quick 2 million dollars in ransom money from his father.

Eastwood has his character toy with a cigar in almost every scene and it's distracting – like a kid's idea of a performance. A murderous sidekick / lover of Strom's is Liesl (Sonia Braga – is she German too?). Braga is a formidable physical presence but has little to say. She has a sex scene with Eastwood; he's tied up to a chair and she cuts him with a razor. It's all meaninglessly lurid. Lara Flynn Boyle shows up as David's wife Sarah for a standard cop's wife cameo.

True Crime – 1999

Around the time of *Bronco Billy* in 1980, Eastwood would occasionally shift from his usual dour self and begin smiling, talking, and offering a more natural demeanor on screen. This didn't improve his line readings or his comedic timing. The connection between the words he was reciting and the intended emotional effects could still seem wildly uneven. The effort - in *Honkytonk Man*, *A Perfect World*, *Bridges of Madison County* and *Absolute Power* - was like a weak stand-in holding down a part while the other actors acted circles around him. This continues in *True Crime*. Eastwood sometimes seems like a drifter who's wandered into his own film. He's unflappable, barely emotional, carefree while everybody else is focused on the dire stakes at play.

The action in *True Crime* takes place in a single day. At midnight, Frank Beechum (Isaiah Washington), a convicted murderer responsible for the death of a pregnant store clerk during an armed robbery, is scheduled to be executed. Eastwood plays Steve Everett, a news writer for the *Oakland Tribune*. He is told to go to San Quentin and write a human-interest byline on Beechum's last day. In preparation, Everett reviews the case and begins to think Beechum is innocent. The few clues will all come without much strain: at one point an address Everett needs from a gigantic trove of papers sort of just shows up on the floor; at another point a woman Everett is questioning suddenly clutches a necklace she is wearing and Everett ties it to the murder from years earlier.

There is a lot of unnecessary nonsense going on around the edges of the film. There is banter about women's liberation of the sort that was stupid back in the seventies and reeked of unrepentent misogyny by 1999. Everett's editor, Bob Findley, is played by Denis Leary. Everett is screwing Findley's wife. Everett's boss at the tribune, Alan Mann, is played by James Woods and it's a horrible performance. In an excruciatingly bad scene, Mann and Everett discuss the wives they have "screwed." Woods shouts, screams, leers and almost foams at the mouth (the queasy quality recalls the scene with the kidnapped highway patrolman in *The Gauntlet* - the dirty words are supposed to be entertaining). Woods plays the part so boisterously his voice carries out onto the work floor, but the news department doesn't seem to notice.

In addition to Everett screwing the editor's young wife, the movie begins with Everett hitting on a 23-year-old fellow reporter and the movie ends with Everett hitting on a young store clerk. Eastwood was 69 years old when he directed and acted in *True Crime* and he still considered womanizing pathologies to be charming. All of Everett's adultery comes at the expense of his wife Barbara (Diane Venora) and their very young daughter Kate (Francesca Eastwood). Venora gives a wonderful acting effort during a scene in the Everett home when the couple is breaking up - she shows the modulated emotion of a woman breaking down. Eastwood looks like he's about to fall asleep on the couch.

There is a heart to the movie though - it lies with Isaiah Washington as the convicted murderer Frank Beechum. Beechum is a born-again Christian with a steadfast wife and daughter, and he's resigned to dying. You find yourself pulling for him even when you're not sure if he committed the crime.

The movie pushes against the death penalty, but I doubt if Eastwood would admit to being against the death penalty. The misogyny is consistent; the death penalty a fleeting plot point.

Space Cowboys – 2000

There is some kind of astronaut deficiency on Mother Earth so NASA has to turn to geriatric ex-astronauts, pull them out of retirement, and send them into outer space to fix a nuclear reactor that has gone out of whack before it comes crashing back to earth endangering everyone. The "astronauts" are played, superficially, by Eastwood, James Garner and Donald Sutherland.

Watching these guys train for the mission is gruesome. They seem to be jogging on the verge of very real heart attacks. The sight reminds us that Eastwood runs like a girl – arms extended, hands sort of flopping upside down while bouncing lightly on a prancing gait as if he fears activating a hernia. These guys don't look any healthier after all the training. We also get to enjoy the sight of these old fellas chasing after women and generally acting like school kids. It will be no surprise to mention that there is no "science" in the film – it's not that kind of cinematic enterprise.

The big climax is dispatched so quickly – seemingly with a wrench and screwdriver atop a phony set design – the whole thing crashes down onto the movie audience endangering everyone.

Gran Torino – 2008

Eastwood is Walt Kowalski, a time-weathered Korean War veteran living alone in the aftermath of his wife's death. Walt is one of the few remaining white people in a neighborhood that is now inhabited by a large number of Hmong - a Laotian / Chinese community who have immigrated into his small Midwestern town. Despite his loudly displayed and virulent racism, Walt becomes friendly with the teenage Hmong boy and girl who live next door to him - Thao (Bee Vang) and Sue (Ahney Her).

When a violent Hmong gang beat-up Thao and steal his work tools, Walt goes to the gang's hangout, beats up one of the gang members and warns him to stay away from Thao.

A compelling sequence follows that suggests what Eastwood's auteur status would be like if he could shake himself free from pandering to white audiences:

Walt's confrontation with the gang has an unintended consequence: it leads to an assault on the family he was trying to protect. A decrepit Walt hears shots and stumbles out of his house. He sees a car rushing away. He makes his way to Thao's house and finds Thao hurt and the family traumatized. Sue is not there. The family begins to worry about Sue. Walt remains with the family late into the night. Finally, Sue stumbles in, raped and badly beaten. As the family consoles her, Walt returns to his home talking to himself, verbally cursing himself, admitting that he screwed up and recognizing that he was responsible for the attack. He sits on the couch in his dark living room and moans. Walt's pathos is moving - a brutal vigilante facing the consequences of his recklessness.

Almost everything else about *Gran Torino* is a fraud - not least the myth of the lovable racist. Never explained is why the Hmong never turn anybody into the police when they know the perpetrators and know where they live. Nor is it explained why the many Hmong men glimpsed in the film don't take any action. Only Walt the racist can save them.

Walt is dying of natural causes, but has kept it to himself. Having nothing to lose, he decides to go back and once again confront the gang. It's dark. He stands in their yard ominously. They see Walt, become alarmed, and begin pulling out guns, semi-automatic weapons, etc. Walt pretends to draw a weapon from his coat. The gang opens fire and kills him.   The cops come and arrest the whole gang because they have killed an unarmed man (he didn't really have a gun). None of the gang - let alone all of them - have thought to flee. What happens when some of them get released on bail? Certainly, some of the gang will get off - those who might not have fired their guns for instance?   The kid who got beat up by Walt previously and saw him with a gun could plead self-defense. With Walt dead, it doesn't mean Thao's family is safe. They might be worse off. Walt's screwed up again because the white supremacist martyr superhero with the heart-of-lead has died without killing the Monster. The superhero must kill the Monster or the community is doomed.

It's a wonder you can be moved by a fleeting sequence in a movie with as much bullshit as this one. Walt seems to be hated by everyone. He can never think of a kind thing to say to his sons, his niece, his neighbors, his priest, his barber. At one point, he confesses to a war crime, reminiscing about shooting a Korean kid in the face when the kid was trying to surrender. His discourse is a string of epithets - gooks, slants, kikes, spooks, cheap Jews, etc. He is disgusted by the Hmong

- how they have let his neighborhood go to hell, their manners, their language, their "being."

The first time, early in the movie, the gang gets into a fight at Thao's house and the violence spills over towards Walt's house. He grabs his rifle and orders them to "get out of my yard." In doing so, he saves Thao. The Hmong community show their respect by bringing him food and flowers. It's a fantasy conversion from lifelong racism to faux-comedic racist banter because the Hmong food smells good and Walt is hungry. In a scene that equals in distaste scenes with James Woods in *True Crime* and scenes with the hi-jacked sheriff in *The Gauntlet*, Walt and his barber Martin (John Carroll Lynch) try to teach Thao how to talk racist, how to talk dirty. It's a big joke if a white man is jiving with another white man, but likely to get Thao killed if he wanders into the wrong ethnic group or into the wrong white group. In this movie, Walt tries to make Thao "a man." What makes you a man is a gun, dirty words, racial insensitivity and a job (one vague reason Walt justifies racism in general is because he worked at the Ford plant for forty years and this particular American dream should have kept his neighborhood white).

It's somewhat revealing that Walt never drops the N-word once in the course of this expletive ridden film. The friendly/racist angle is played both ways. But never realistically.

The religious aspect is also suspect. Walt's wife was close to the Catholic church. Father Janovich (Christopher Carley) tries to honor her last wishes by guiding Walt to confession, but Walt is stubborn. He hates the church, the hypocrisy, etc. Finally, he caves in and confesses. The confession is a doozy: he kissed a girl once when he was married and he wished he'd been closer to his sons.

In interviews, Eastwood actually bragged about offering a *not-politically-correct* movie to his audience. Is he really saying: anti-racism is politically correct but I have the courage to be a racist?

Invictus – 2009

After 27 years, Nelson Mandela (Morgan Freeman), a legend to black South Africans, is released from prison. Soon elected as South Africa's president, Mandela has to deal with healing the wounds of the ex-apartheid nation. Rejecting the revenge strategies that are rising up in some quarters, he strives towards unifying black and white citizens. As Mandela attempts to speak to South Africa as a one-people nation, he seizes upon the idea of supporting the South African "Green and Gold," all-white-minus-one, rugby team fronted by team captain Francois Pienaar (Matt Damon). The team, heading toward the 1995 Rugby World Cup, is beloved by white South Africans and somewhat reviled by black South Africans. Mandela uses the team as a ploy to push the country towards a united front.

Morgan Freeman recites his lines so sententiously it probably adds an extra ten minutes to the film. As he argues with the white African leadership, his daughters, his constituents – everything is stated in much too gentlemanly a manner. Issues of race are toned down almost to invisibility as the sports plot asserts itself. Most of the dramatic focus is on team captain Pienaar, a well-educated and upscale Afrikaner, as he begins to recognize the extent of Mandela's sacrifice and the importance of his unification effort. The only moving moment comes when Pienaar visits the small cell that held Mandela for years and he gets a glimpse of what his life must have been like.

By the time the movie gets to the big sports event – the Green and Gold against the All Blacks (a Maori team dressed in black) – there isn't much time left to do the game justice. As somebody who doesn't know rugby – the scoring seemed to ebb and flow unnaturally and the teams are constantly in a penalty huddle of some sort. The camera placement strikes me as completely inept – like the movie-makers couldn't afford the time or effort to capture the game adequately. More importantly, there is never any clear indication of how the games brought anybody together in any way that seems convincing. As a result, *Invictus* ends up being a romanticized story about rugby.

Hereafter - 2010

When he was very young, George Lonegan (Matt Damon) suffered a serious spinal infection, became gravely ill, and almost gave up the ghost. The near-death experience left Lonegan with the gift / curse of clairvoyance. Just the touch of a fellow human being (it comes with a "Whoooosh" sound) allows him instantaneous contact with their dearly departed, and he can successfully channel messages from the afterlife. Living in San Francisco, working in a factory, Lonegan has given up using clairvoyance as a means to make money because, as he says, "he needs to quit dealing with death and begin to deal with life." His brother Billy (Jay Mohr) doesn't understand his reluctance and wants him to cash in on his unique skill.

Marie Lelay (Cecile de France) a popular French television newscaster appears to be on an excursion in Indonesia with her boss Didier (Thierry Neuvic). Marie leaves Didier in their hotel room and goes out into the streets to buy a gift for his children. Didier is awakened by screams and a roaring sound. He gets up, looks out of his hotel window and sees the ocean receding violently. Then he sees the waves returning in great height and they roll over the beach, flooding everything as the hotel begins to shake. In the street, Marie has also heard the roar and she sees the gigantic waves in the distance heading her way. She grabs a young girl. They run, but are hit by the deluge, knocked about, and tumbled with great violence. Marie loses her grip and the girl disappears into the deluge. Marie struggles in the water. She manages to climb onto a piece of refuse but a tossed-about car hits her and knocks her unconscious. Left floating beneath the water, Marie experiences a bright light and a vision of dark figures walking in partial darkness. She is fished out of the water, pulled to dry land, and attempts are made to rescue her. She is given up for dead. She experiences more visions before suddenly reviving and coughing up water.

Over in England, the 12-year-old twins Marcus and Jason (Frankie and George McLaren) are living with their heroin addict mother Jackie (Lyndsey Marshal) who is being hounded by social workers. After a rough, drugged-out night, Jackie decides to go straight and sends Jason to the druggist for some anti-addiction medicine. On the way back from the store Jason is struck and killed by a car. His brother Marcus is devastated. As a result, his mother is put in rehab and Marcus is placed in foster care.

Towards the end of the movie, Marie from France, Lonegan from San Francisco and Marcus will all meet by coincidence in London. Lonegan will be there after he is laid off from his job - he is a great fan of Charles Dickens and has always wanted to go to London to see the Dickens' House. He notices that Derek Jacobi will be doing a reading of Dickens at a book fair so he heads for the fair.

Marie has been shaken up by the disaster and obsessed with her visions. She is supposed to be taking time off from her French news job to recuperate and write a book about Francois Mitterrand, but instead becomes more interested in writing about near-death experiences; her book, entitled *Hereafter,* is published and she is going to London to read at the book fair.

Young Marcus has become withdrawn and increasingly obsessed with the death of his brother (he wears his brother's baseball cap or keeps it by his side at all times). Marcus researches "the afterlife" on his computer and studies the writings of psychics and mediums. He steals a large amount of money from his foster parents and begins a search for a psychic who can contact his brother. He meets a bunch of frauds. Disenchanted he wanders into the book fair and recognizes George Lonegan as one of the psychics he has seen online.

Now this may seem like a lot happens; and it could suggest a very interesting story; but after the first ten minutes of film time - which comprises the tsunami - *Hereafter* is dead as a doorknob.

There are a multitude of problems:

1. At the book fair Lonegan asks Marie for her autograph. As she hands the book to him, he brushes her hand and "Whooosh" he gets a glimpse of her "vision." He backs away, realizing she is like him in some way. At the same time, Marcus spots Lonegan and begins pestering him, desperately telling him he needs to talk. Marie hears Marcus refer to Lonegan as a psychic. Marcus's nagging makes Lonegan flee and when he returns Marie is gone. Marcus sneakily follows Lonegan to his hotel. Lonegan finally agrees to give Marcus a reading. He touches Marcus and we hear the sound, and he tells Marcus that Jason is with him always, yada yada yada. Marcus feels better and that's the end of his problem.

2. Later, Marcus calls Lonegan at his hotel and says he has found Marie's phone number. Lonegan arranges a meeting with Marie at an outdoor café. He sees her approaching in the crowd. He has a daydream of kissing her. She almost doesn't see him. Then she does. Lonegan approaches her. He shakes her hand. There is no "Whooossh."

3. The film never knows what it is or what it is supposed to be saying. Eastwood had stated his interest in filming a supernatural story, but it doesn't fall into any category that is supernatural friendly: it's not supernatural horror, it's not a supernatural mystery, it's not supernatural comedy. It plays like a weird docu-drama where all the events are supposedly true. The protagonists complain about a "conspiracy to silence them." They insist that proof of life after death is "irrefutable" (this comes in a cheesy scene in a mental ward with a creepy psychiatrist). What the movie actually depicts is the real-life trauma of Post-Traumatic Stress Disorder. Luis Bunuel, Ingmar Berman films, even David Fincher films all suggest ways spiritual / trauma themes could be handled in a compelling manner, but *Hereafter* is pure nonsense.

4. Many of the individual scenes are horrible. Eastwood has no interest in depicting the newsroom sequences accurately - Marie is supposed to be a host on a popular news show but the scenes play like the most boring chit-chat on local city-run community broadcasts. In a London subway, young Marcus is trying to get on a train, but Jason's hat blows off of his head and he takes some time trying to retrieve it from amongst the feet of the moving crowd. Marcus just misses getting into the train. As he backs away, the train moves into a tunnel. A gigantic explosion is heard as a bomb rips apart the train (Jason's brother's hat has saved him - but not so much the passengers).

5. When Marcus goes online to check out ideas about death, he gets a roster of equal opportunity Islamic and Christian opinions about the afterlife. They are all dismissed by Marcus as bogus. Why is Lonegan the only one who has anything real to offer? Seeing Lonegan in action he looks like just another average medium.

6. The soundtrack is Eastwood tinkling around on the keyboard with portentous sounding imbecility.

Hereafter did okay at the box office but received critically mixed reviews. A look at Peter Travers and Robert Ebert's comments shows how strained the superlative reviewers can get when trying to defend crap.

Travers: "In more than half a century of making movies, Clint Eastwood, 80, has sent many a varmint to his maker. *Hereafter* is the first time he's showed any curiosity about what lies on the other side. It's typical of Eastwood's mastery as a director that his approach to the topic is introspective, not inflammatory. *Hereafter*, set to a resonant Eastwood score, truly is haunting.

Hereafter isn't any more interested about what's "on the other side" than any of Eastwood's men-with-no-name-from-hell-or-heaven movies. These types of movies aren't supposed to be *serious* attempts at philosophy or theology. And who the hell would Eastwood possibly be "inflaming" by not treating an unserious subject seriously? Psychics? Conspiracy nuts? What in the world is supernatural introspection anyway?

Travers does share a little of the very bad news: "Eastwood hits narrative bumps on this atypical spiritual journey, as does politics-obsessed screenwriter Peter Morgan (*The Queen*; *Frost / Nixon*). No worries. It's exhilarating to watch these two talents explore new ground without bias or trendy cynicism."

Hereafter is not an "atypical" film, it's a foolish one. This is not "new" ground for anybody. It's a make-a-buck supernatural film in the supernatural genre that manages to be boring as hell.

Roger Ebert's comments were even more perplexing: "I don't believe in woo-woo, but then neither, I suspect, does Eastwood. This is a film for intelligent people who are naturally curious about what happens when the shutters close. It is the film of a man at peace. He has nothing to prove except his care for the living." Say what? An intelligent film about "woo-woo." And what's this "care for the living" nonsense. Say that to most of Eastwood's characters and they'd probably shoot you with a gun. Punk.

The Empty Chair
August 30, 2012 Republican National Convention

Clint Eastwood has given a lot of mediocre performances: *Outlaw Josey Wales*, *The Rookie*, *A Perfect World*, among them. He has given even more bad performances of which I'd cite the following: the lecherous, misogynist, homophobic, racist, "professor of art" in *The Eiger Sanction*; the alcoholic, armed robber / terrorist, "country-western" role model for child neglect in *Honkytonk Man*; the morally decadent version of Dirty Harry carried to another silly extreme in *Sudden Impact*; the wallowing-in-excess as a Marine in the horrid *Heartbreak Ridge*; the "what-the-hell-was-that" imitation of John Huston in *White Hunter, Black Heart*; the emotionless romantic foil in *Bridges of Madison County*; the senile macho poser in *Space Cowboys*.

Joining this list was Eastwood's turn as a speaker at the Republican National Convention in August, 2012 in support of Mitt Romney.

Eastwood is not known for his improvisatory talents. He is also not a deep thinker - on politics, on cinema, on social justice. Eastwood's RNC speech began with an inarticulate ramble that would be sustained for countless minutes. An empty chair had been placed beside the podium and Eastwood began addressing the chair as if President Obama were sitting in it. Eastwood hectored the chair. He put words into the chair's mouth that the chair would never in his beatific grace have uttered. In a roundabout way, Eastwood's Obama-ghost tells Mitt Romney to "f**k himself." Eastwood chides the chair and "the chair" tells him to "go f**k himself" - to which Eastwood replies "but that's impossible."

An ill-placed slippage of the tongue, an untoward "boy" inserted somewhere in the ramble might have revealed the speech for what it was to those viewers who tend to miss such things. Romney strategist Stuart Stevens who cleared Eastwood to speak at the convention reportedly threw up while watching the spectacle. Republicans who didn't want to offend moderates (this was back in the day when Republicans were worried about offending moderates) were guarded in their assessments, but appreciated that Eastwood was great for the rancid side of the base.

Eastwood has always been a great pretender. Early on in his career he pretended not to see the many anti-humanitarian strains in his films. He would argue that critics who saw "fascism" in his stories didn't know what they were talking about. He feigned innocence of the ideas he was throwing up onscreen, just like people feigned innocence when suggesting that Obama was born in Kenya (even when they knew Obama wasn't born in Kenya), or that Hillary Clinton was running a pedophilia ring out of a pizza restaurant. Even though Eastwood has spoken consistently down the years about how much he didn't like the hippies, the Me Generation, the X Generation, the Millennials - how no generation has lived up to his grand expectations - critics have been reluctant to call him out for being a cranky bastard with a challenged world view.

In a way similar to Donald Trump, Eastwood's speech at the convention was pure projection - smothering President Obama with the stark failure Eastwood possibly felt as a man. The dirty-talk shoved on the President is likely the kind of talk that comes out of Eastwood's own mouth. Perhaps at home he has the same kind of imaginary conversations with a chair and the ghost of Pauline Kael.

Projecting his self-pride as a successful businessman, Eastwood suggested the country needed a businessman like Romney for President. As if George W. Bush, the torture president, the lie-yourself-into-a-war President, and the worst economy since the Great Depression President hadn't already shown the downside of a businessman for the highest office. It should be remembered that Eastwood's own short term as a politician was an aborted job as Mayor of Carmel. Somewhat like Sarah Palin, he decided to quit the job early so he could get back to more lucrative endeavors.

The creepiest part of Eastwood's convention speech was the delivery of the line, "Politicians don't own us - we own them - they do what we tell them to - they come around begging every few years..." Seemingly intended as a we-the-people throwaway, it came off as a blunt acknowledgement that the Republican business class thinks they own the leaders of the country.

Eastwood also ran through a list of complaints about President Obama - jobs, closing Guantanamo, world respect, the economy. You get an idea of Eastwood as suggested by his films: a Republican on the tea party side of things.

It's hard to fathom how an astute critic like David Denby can defend Eastwood by calling his politics "social liberal, fiscally conservative." It's been a long time since the latter hasn't obliterated the former in Conservative politics. Eastwood tries to hide his views behind a "Libertarian" banner whenever he is pressed (suggesting, you know, that he is against both sides and has a different, more superior, view of things). If Eastwood were anything other than a right-wing pontificator, if he were truly just being "not politically correct" - as he has boasted about, most recently in an interview regarding *Gran Torino* - the result would be double-edged like Howard Stern or Frank Zappa or *Saturday Night Live* - disdain thrown everywhere - not just towards those damn liberals and their colored friends.

If you listen closely, you can hear the subtexts in Eastwood's voice:

"Everybody's walking on eggshells. We see people accusing people of being racist and all kinds of stuff. When I grew up, those things weren't called racist."

Is he talking about "things" like blackface, voter suppression, demeaning language, the "N" word (which Eastwood has never dared to use in his films because it would signify the obvious), unequal pay, segregated schools, nationalism, white supremacy, cops murdering black people? Actually, these are the same things people are calling racist now that were racist then – Eastwood's feigned stupidity isn't persuasive.

It isn't surprising that Eastwood has been a Trump supporter: He puts it this way, "You know, 'cause [Hillary's] declared that she's gonna follow in Obama's footsteps." Eastwood added about Hillary: "It's a tough voice to listen to for four years." Another "not politically correct" statement that means he prefers to hear a man's voice even if it is as colorless as his own. Eastwood notes that Trump has "said a lot of dumb things" but he thinks that voters need to "just … get over it".

Eastwood finally got his businessman for President - how's that going for you Clint? "Well, I think Trump is on to something … critics should just shut up - he won the election."

If Eastwood has an artistic persona at all, this is it.

American Sniper – 2014

American Sniper is a horrible film to contemplate. I've watched it four times trying to figure out why it is so offensive. What I've settled on is that the batch of thought processes wasted on the film's conception are at hopeless cross-purposes. Based to some extent on Chris Kyle's Iraq War memoir with the Trumpian braggadocio title of *American Sniper: The Autobiography of the Most Lethal Sniper in U.S. Military History*, the story was subsequently hyped up by a slew of actors, writers and directors with different ideas about what they wanted to say. On top of that, Chris Kyle had to be trusted as a narrator. Given some of the repulsion that's greeted Kyle's statements about Iraqis, and controversy over his claims of how many medals he earned – the source material leaves too much of the vetting of veracity to Kyle himself – in both Iraq and at home. Steven Spielberg was set to direct at one time and there may be a lost movie in here somewhere – a movie much better than the finished product about how the Iraqi resistance was to some extent a mirror of the US occupation forces – sniper to sniper, brutality to brutality, moral bs to moral bs, patriot to patriot. Bradley Cooper, who bought the rights to Kyle's book, had a different idea when responding to critics of the film; he stated: "We looked at hopefully igniting attention about the lack of care that goes to vets." But this is another lost cause: the film is not about vets, or their "lack of care," and the only screen time given to the subject in its 132-minute running time is probably about 10 minutes.

Eastwood was no help – he called it an "anti-war" film though that is hardly what is on the screen – any contextualizing of the Iraq War from any counter-viewpoint than that of Kyle and / or the fictional Kyle is largely absent. Directorial presence is so lacking this may as well have been, to some extent, a directorial effort by Kyle himself with most of the implicit self-interest intact.

Early scenes show Chris Kyle as a boy. His father teaches him to hunt. When Chris kills a deer, his father tells him he has "a gift." When bullies beat up his younger brother, Kyle's dad rants about how people are either sheep (victims), wolves (evil), or sheepdogs (they protect the sheep victims). His father pulls off his belt and threatens punishment if his sons ever become "wolves." Kyle says he won't; his father replies – "good, you know what you are" – meaning a sheepdog. This flimsy black / white edifice might have been challenged in a Spielberg film. Eastwood, on the other hand, doesn't seem to have rejected any of the ideas that popped up during the film's conception and the competing viewpoints are perplexing.

We meet an older Chris Kyle as part of a rodeo. He drinks beer and is fairly shiftless. He wants to be a cowboy – whatever that was in those days. His beer-addled brain contemplates a television newscast showing the terrorist bombing in 1998 at US Embassies in Tanzania and Kenya which killed hundreds, including 12 Americans. Kyle takes umbrage saying "Look what they done to us" before sinking back into beer-faced oblivion. Years later, he will take further umbrage when a television newscast shows the fall of the Twin Towers on 9/11. In fact, he gets so mad he decides to go fight them, not in Saudi Arabia where they were from, but in Iraq (chasing those "weapons of mass destruction" though it seems forbidden to bring up any Iraq War pushback in this film).

I don't really get Bradley Cooper's approach. At times, the performance seems like a parody of Kyle. Cooper beefed up considerably for this film but he doesn't look strong – he just looks thick – meat sort of floating all around his body. The thickness extends to Kyle's head as well. His version of Kyle takes in everything with a befuddled glaze, even when he isn't drinking. There are several instances in the film where Kyle tries to formulate ideas, but they never quite make it to the exotic land of reason before falling back into blurry senescence.

Eastwood is clearly responsible for the lazy Navy Seal training scenes which show soldiers getting sprayed with a hose while they are doing set-ups, or spooning with other trainees in the mud, or lying in "53 degree" ocean water. We will take the script's word for it that Kyle was somewhat romantic when wooing his soon-to-be bride Taya (Sienna Miller). Taya gets pregnant and Kyle is off to Iraq for his first tour of duty.

The movie actually starts with a short sequence in Iraq which sets up a moral dilemma. Kyle and a soldier are on a rooftop; Kyle is surveying the streets with his rifle's telescope. A woman and a young boy emerge from a building and immediately Kyle notices the woman is walking stiffly like she is carrying something under her clothes. He relays the information. The soldier with him cautions him, if he makes a mistake, "you could end up in Leavenworth." The woman stops, carefully removes a hand grenade, and gives it to the boy. The boy begins walking towards an American tank and troops. Kyle shoots and kills the kid. The woman runs towards the child, picks up the grenade and is shot in the act of throwing it. The grenade makes a huge explosion. Kyle is congratulated – this is his first kill.

It's distressing to find out the child wasn't actually part of the real Kyle's first killing – the kid was added during the script process. If you are going to hype moral dilemmas against the truth you might as well hype them all over, and any close look at this film shows an ongoing inattention to rectitude. For instance, many people would state the moral dilemma shown here is connected to actions of politicians back in the USA who pushed troops into Iraq based on false claims of weapons of mass destruction, and false claims of immediate threats to the United States using 9/11 as a pretext. The beginning sequence with the mother / child is blind to that particular moral dilemma – for instance, the possible moral anguish an Iraqi woman might have had about dragging her son along to throw grenades at American troops isn't part of the equation. You might also notice that the fear of "Leavenworth" itself is a hyped-up fear. We can assume some innocent people were killed in Iraq, but how many actual soldiers are in Leavenworth or any other US prison for killing Iraqi civilians?

Let's look at *American Sniper* for what it is. This is an American war hero movie gone wrong. This is not a winning the hearts and minds of Iraq movie. When Kyle goes back for his second tour he is escorted in a helicopter and discusses the "savages" with his commander – he has become a cowboy and the Iraqis are the Indians. The "savages" subject is brought up again along with a Zale's Jewelry commercial when Kyle is out on patrol with his friend Biggles (Jake McDorman). Earlier in the film Kyle's unit was told to go door to door and shake up some information about a guy referred to as "the Butcher" (Mido Hamada). They seem to use very little discrimination in busting down doors. The soldiers home-invade a family and terrorize them. They scream and push their rifles into the faces of a young boy and the men and women in the house. They demand information and an old man calls over one of the women. She shows Kyle her arm; it has been cut off from the elbow down – by the Butcher – this family isn't friendly with the Butcher. The soldiers push the man to give them information. A few scenes later the Butcher has come back and suspects collusion. He kills the child in the street and shoots the old man. It's hard not to see some of the responsibility for the deaths of the father and son residing with the American soldiers, but in this movie this kind of morality isn't an issue.

The Butcher was not an actual real-life person. Same with the Iraqi sniper Mustapha (Sammy Sheik) – who is Kyle's sniper nemesis. Mustapha is offing American soldiers at roughly the same rate Kyle offs Iraqis. Mustapha is a deadly shot. He will be responsible for the maiming of Kyle's friend Biggles. The Marines make Mustapha a top priority. Kyle, shooting one of his longest shots ever, manages to kill him. The real Kyle will say this is not how it happened – he killed somebody else with his longest shot ever. Mustapha is also "based" on somebody. This sorting out of reality becomes an offshoot of watching the film. The Butcher and Mustapha are offered as Hollywood villains in order to run a consistent thread of suspense through Kyle's four deployments.

The first scene of the movie where Kyle decides whether to shoot the child and the woman is tied to another scene. Kyle is on a rooftop chalking up his kills. Through his gun's scope he sees a man emerge from the shadows with a grenade launcher. It happens fast, Kyle is caught slightly off-guard. The man raises the weapon to shoot at American troops. Kyle manages to get off a shot and kill him. But a young child has been sitting nearby and sees the man shot down. He runs over. He struggles to pick up the grenade launcher – it is bigger than he is. Kyle keeps his trigger finger ready, but is anguished – "don't do it" he says to himself. And just before Kyle shoots him, the boy throws down the weapon and runs away to safety. This is supposed to resolve any questions that we may have about Kyle ever killing an innocent person.

One of the failures of this movie is the way it forces you to appraise Chris Kyle's sniper prowess and the general veracity of the events depicted. It leaves you with ugly questions. The reporting seems suspect: "255 kills, with 160 of them confirmed by the Pentagon." I'm not really certain what this means. Who is doing the counting? The same people who added up the casualties in Vietnam? How are they "confirmed." And how accurate is that? Does making sniping a sport increase left-handed shooting, so to speak? There is a stray line in the film when Kyle does soft push-back on accolades about his sniping skills and an officer tells him essentially to shut-up "the troops *need to think* they are protected." The "truth" about Kyle isn't necessary. When the film's Kyle says he's certain that the sniper shooting at them from about a mile away is Mustapha – would he have really been certain if he hadn't seen Mustapha in close-ups like the audience does? When Kyle sits down and talks to a psychiatrist about what he's done, he professes that he can go before God and validate every one of his killings – given that he considers the Iraqi "savages" – isn't he setting the bar kind of low on what he considers fair game? And given the black / white emphasis on wolves / sheep / sheepdog – does it really matter since all the Iraqis are wolves?

Cooper's portrayal of Kyle is stone cold. At one point Kyle meets his younger brother in Iraq when his brother is heading home. Kyle is happy to see him, but his brother is shaking, distracted, nervous – he just wants to get on the plane. "Fuck this place," he tells Kyle. Kyle stares at him like he's seeing a mortal enemy. Whatever Kyle is registering in his head isn't friendly. He is repulsed. In another scene in Iraq, Kyle is briefly confronted by his friend Mark Lee (Luke Grimes). Earlier Lee had tried to cool down Kyle's gung-ho attitude – asking Kyle if he has some kind of "savior complex." During Kyle's second tour, the same character asks Kyle if he has "a god." "Of course, I have a god. You getting weird on me?" Lee says, "I just want to believe in what we're doing here." Kyle tells him there is evil there – they've seen it. "There's evil everywhere," Lee replies. Kyle says, "Do you want these motherfuckers to come to San Diego or New York." As Lee walks away we are left with another Cooper trance-like stare suggesting incomprehension with Mark Lee's stupidity. The sickliest aspect of this film is the way it uses the real Chris Kyle's experience to try to foist an idea of blind patriotism down the audience's throat without showing any collateral damage – Cooper's professed good intentions to the contrary. Eastwood's Kyle is the ideal man for any war machine and any God anywhere. He *is* Mustapha.

All of this plays against Bradley Cooper's suggestion that this has something to do with veterans, what they endure in the war and what they bring home to their families. Kyle didn't seem all that friendly at the beginning of the movie when he was punching out people and kicking his girlfriend out of his house. Throughout the film he appears shut down, avoidant, isolated from reality, only coming into his own with some degree of confidence when he starts being referred to as The Legend among his fellow soldiers.

Eastwood is disingenuous comparing this film to "another film I made, *Letters from Iwo Jima* – which was about people being plucked for war?" Kyle wasn't drafted – this was a volunteer army. The unexpected and unwanted redeployments that many troops and their families suffered were a hallmark of the bad planning of this particular war – it was supposed to last a couple of months and the savages were supposed to greet the Army as liberators – but this is not a concern of the film either.

If you isolate the scenes where Kyle returns home you get the following:

1. First time back, Taya is close to having a baby. Kyle doesn't talk much, seems despondent. Taya calls him out about it. A nurse at the hospital where Taya is getting a checkup asks how Kyle is "decompressing". He says fine.

She takes his blood pressure – it's 170/110. This is reminiscent of *The Hurt Locker* – the return home is depicted as one in which the soldier suffers a postpartum depression – he wants to be back at war and he can't settle down. On their way home from the hospital Kyle starts complaining about how nobody acts like there is a war going on, he needs to get back (I'm not sure how we are supposed to take this – the war was controversial on a daily basis, maybe Kyle didn't watch the news). Kyle's outburst is interrupted when Taya goes into labor. Later, Kyle is watching videos from Iraq that depict American soldiers being shot – videos the enemy "gives away on the street" Kyle tells Taya. He blames Mustapha. Mustapha is still loose so he needs to go back. Taya keeps trying to bring Kyle back to the here and now, almost snapping her fingers in his face, trying to make him focus. He cannot resist the call of the sheepdog.

2. After the second tour, Taya continues to notice Kyle is shut down. She tells him "If you don't think this war is changing you, you're wrong." He runs into a soldier he saved in Iraq who lost a leg. The soldier thanks Kyle, but when Kyle asks him if he lost friends, he says he worries about the survivors, who "haven't come back" (meaning the wounded). He invites Kyle to the VA hospital but Kyle is indifferent.

3. During his third tour his friend Biggles had been badly wounded by "Mustapha" and Mark Lee has been killed. Back home at Lee's funeral his mother reads a skeptical anti-war letter from Lee written two weeks before he was killed. When Taya asks Kyle what he thought of the letter, he says Lee's letter is what "killed him." He shouldn't have let himself go. Kyle visits Biggles in the hospital and tells him he's going to go back to Iraqi to get revenge for what Mustapha did to him.

4. During his fourth tour of duty the action hero part of the movie is neatly tied up. Kyle kills the fictional "Mustapha" and finally starts to show some war fatigue when he's pinned down in a violent attack. He returns home, seems lost, withdrawn and haunted. After an incident at a barbeque when he becomes unnaturally violent towards a dog – he decides to visit the VA. He is interviewed by a psychiatrist who probes him about things "he may have seen" that disturb him. Kyle says he just feels guilty because he is still able to fight, but is not back helping the troops – once again an American film depicting the vast array of problems with PTSD as a simple heroic desire to be back in battle. The psychiatrist tells him "There are plenty of soldiers who need saving right here" – meaning in the hospital. It is at this point that Kyle starts interacting with vets.

These sequences are squashed together and heavily streamlined and embedded with the general ending of the film. Kyle jokes with some bedridden vets and starts coaching vets at the rifle range.

The NRA must have chipped in some money on the ending because various scenes are filled with guns. We get a sequence with Kyle out hunting with his young son which echo the early scenes with Kyle's father. Kyle tells him, "It's not easy to stop a heartbeat for the first time," but encourages him to not back down – and it's also a creepy reference to Kyle's first kill in Iraq. There are times when this film seems to be laughing at this fictional Kyle – like he stands in for every unquestioning soldier everywhere and their propagation of even more unquestioning soldiers. Same with another scene at the end where Kyle and his kid creep through the house with Kyle holding a toy cowboy six-shooter (though it seems a deluxe model). He sneaks into the kitchen, holds the gun on his wife and says "drop your drawers." Kyle has once again become the cowboy he's always wanted to be, but

Eastwood's film is so oblivious to its own metaphors that the obvious Native American rape transgression suggested here could not possibly have been registered in the filmmakers' mind.

Another gun shows up, this time with Kyle and a wounded vet out shooting targets. When the vet makes a good shot he says, "Yeah, I feel like I got my balls back." There are times when I think the film is just toying with us.

The last scene shows Kyle meeting up with another vet he's taking to the rifle range. This will be the vet that kills Kyle.

The film ends with archival footage showing Chris Kyle's funeral procession making its way down the highway flagged by hundreds of mourners. The footage is quite moving, but actually it is not real footage. It has been doctored up in Hollywood, slowed down in motion, and hung with a mournful score. The reality was something quite different.

The Mule - 2018

The Mule introduces us to Earl Stone (Eastwood), a 78-year-old horticulturist whose forte appears to be orchids. It is 2005 and Earl is attending a flower convention. Earl knows everybody - he's a backslapper. The ladies love him and Earl enjoys the attention. He wins an award for his flower display. Later, in the bar, he buys drinks for everybody. This event is cross-cut with scenes showing the wedding of Earl's daughter Iris (Alison Eastwood). He is missing the wedding because of the convention and we quickly learn that Iris and Earl's ex-wife Mary (Dianne Wiest) have long been estranged from Earl. When he was married to Mary, he largely spent time traveling the country, avoiding home life, philandering, using the business as an excuse.

After these scenes the film jumps to 2017 and the jump feels incongruent because for some reason Earl at 90 years old seems younger. In the intervening years, the rise of internet shopping has driven Earl out of business, so he is packing up the greenhouse in his old pick-up. He decides to attend a party celebrating the engagement and upcoming wedding of his niece Ginny (Taissa Farmiga). The family is shocked to see Earl. Daughter Iris has long ago stopped talking to him. Earl gets into a heated argument with Mary and decides to leave. As he is leaving, a friend of Ginny's tells Earl he has heard Earl likes to drive. He has a job for Earl if he needs the money.

Earl is broke and decides to follow up on the offer. He is surprised to find out he will be moving merchandise for a bunch of mean-looking, gun-toting Hispanics. He has to drive cross-country to Chicago, check into a hotel, leave his car parked for an hour, then go back to his car and he will find cash waiting for him in his glove compartment and the merchandise gone. Earl doesn't ask questions, makes the trip, and gets the money. He is very impressed with the money and sticks with the job.

Eastwood plays the role as alternately senile and sharp. The gang starts to warm up to Earl, humoring him, treating him with respect. Earl finally checks the merchandise and is surprised to find he is toting drugs. But by now he's bought a new truck, been able to attend his niece's wedding with a wad of cash, and the family is starting to warm up a bit, even though he seems a complete womanizer at the wedding.

Earl gets such a great reputation for moving narcotics that a drug kingpin named Laton (Andy Garcia) takes an interest in Earl and wants to start using Earl for major, expensive runs. Laton assigns a young man he has taken under his wing named Julio (Ignacio Serricchio) to shadow Earl, to see if Earl can be trusted. Earl gets Julio out of a jam with police and Julio also begins to like Earl.

Meanwhile, Chicago DEA agents led by Colin Bates (Bradley Cooper) have turned up an informant who begins supplying information on the drug gang.

Laton, the drug kingpin, invites Earl to his mansion. They take a liking to each other and Earl is put up in high style, including two women for a late-night tryst (Earl likes two at a time and has prostitutes on hand at every hotel stop).

Earl attends a graduation ceremony for his niece and learns that his wife Mary is dying.

Laton is murdered by his hired hands. The gang becomes violent and starts putting more pressure on Earl.

Earl learns that Agent Bates is on his trail, even running into him at a restaurant for a short conversation where they bond somewhat without Bates knowing Earl is the man he is after.

Earl visits Mary on her deathbed. He tells her he loves her. She says she appreciates him showing up. His daughter Iris observes this.

Finally, Agent Bates captures Earl on the freeway. This is followed by a short scene in a courtroom where Earl pleads guilty and his family cries.

The fundamental flaw with *The Mule* is the way Eastwood diminishes his character by making everything he does too cute - the drug running, the womanizing, the accepting of gifts from murderers - then making everything spill over into unbelievable sentiment at his wife's deathbed. Eastwood doesn't know this character; he doesn't recognize the bad vibes that spill out from Earl all over the place.

Bradley Cooper barely registers and I'm not sure his partner, played by Michael Pena, is even given a name. Dianne Wiest tries to interject some eccentricity into her scenes but nothing develops. At first, Andy Garcia's Laton is murderous. Later, he becomes endearing for no particular reason. When Laton is murdered without explanation, the director never clarifies the transition from him to his minions. Ignacio Serricchio, who plays Julio, disappears from the film along with most of the other actors. And finally, it's puzzling as to why the family hated Earl back when he had an honest job, but are weeping all over him when they find out he's a drug dealer. The "mule" theme is handled like it isn't a bad job at all, betraying Eastwood's usual hard-on-crime stance.

At one point, the drug dealers figure out that the police are looking for a black truck and I'm still trying to figure out why they didn't get Earl a red car or something.

Andrew Sarris used to refer to "twilight masterpieces" - those films made late in life by directors like Akira Kurosawa, John Ford and Ingmar Bergman that offer a wellspring of cinematic vision and accrued wisdom. By 2018,

Eastwood had been engaging in twilight hackwork for a very long time. *The Mule* continued a tepid string of films "based on true events."

The usual bad product placement is present - *Viagra*, *Google*, *Twitter*, and a horde of car and truck commercials.

Here are two quintessential Eastwood moments from *The Mule*:

First: On one of his drug runs, he pulls over to the side of the road to help an African-American couple with a baby fix their flat tire. The husband doesn't know how to change the tire, he seems stupid and is looking up instructions on *Google*. When Earl says, "I don't mind helping Negroes," the couple gets upset, awkward, and tell Earl they prefer to be called "blacks." Earl makes a joke about this. Really? Eastwood had to go there? Create these fake people unnecessary to the story so he could turn their need for help into an argument about black people biting the hand that feeds them?

Second: Listen to the way Eastwood falls out of character when Agent Collins tells Earl he really likes him because he is "unfiltered." Eastwood gets giddy with the acclimation, responding "I've been unfiltered for years."

Penn Teller recently stated that he liked Donald Trump because he was "unfiltered." Fetching the word for himself, Eastwood seems not to understand the negative implications. His self-reverence is laughable.

MORE

CINEMATIC

FOOLISHNESS

More Cinematic Foolishness

Play Misty for Me – 1971

Play Misty for Me represented a time-honored route for new directors hoping to break into the Hollywood film industry. Low budget horror films, sci-fi films and youth exploitation flicks would help thrust a new wave of American film directors towards secure financial footing. The following are examples from directors who started their careers at roughly the same time as Eastwood:

Steven Spielberg – *Duel.* Spielberg's first full length movie from 1971 – an almost unpopulated suspense film involving a duel to the death between a traveling everyman (Dennis Weaver) and a giant truck. Much is made of very little, including a lot of silence and a crafty use of the soundtrack.

Peter Bogdanovich – *Targets.* A 1968 film with a supporting role from Boris Karloff as a retiring horror-movie star loosely connected to a plot about a lone gunman shooting people at random. Filmed in black and white, the movie includes an eerie sequence of a sniper targeting cars on a freeway – when the drivers are hit the cars coast silently off the road in poetically grim fashion. The movie was made for less than 150,000 dollars.

Brian DePalma – *Greetings* and *Hi, Mom.* Two early films starring Robert De Niro released in 1968 and 1970 – the first involves teenagers trying to avoid being drafted into the Vietnam War; the second is a sequel and uses a variety of self-conscious film techniques DePalma had picked up as a student of Brecht, Godard and Hitchcock. Both films were originally X-rated. Both films were made cheaply – *Greetings* for less than 50,000 dollars.

George Lucas – *THX 1138.* A dystopian science fiction film about a future where sex is prohibited and drugs are mandatory. Made for less than 800,000 dollars. Performed badly at the box office.

Martin Scorsese – *Who's That Knocking at My Door.* Perhaps the most unusual story among the bunch, this is a 1967 film about Catholic guilt starring Harvey Keitel, shot for less than 100,000 dollars.

Francis Ford Coppola – Coppola started directing horror films with producer Roger Corman in the early sixties including *The Terror* and *Dementia 13.* The budget for *Dementia 13* was approximately 50,000 dollars.

William Friedkin – *Good Times* – A 1967 comedy spoofing old movies starring Sonny and Cher. The movie had a fairly high budget – approx. 2 million dollars – but lost money at the box office.

Eastwood's budget for *Play Misty for Me* was more generous than most of these films – close to 1 million dollars. The cinematographer Bruce Surtees was borrowed from Donald Siegel and his work on *Misty* is most striking as a travelogue seemingly financed by the Chamber of Commerce of Carmel, California. Bars and eateries of Carmel are namedropped along the way. The town is stunningly beautiful and much of the plot takes a back seat to the wind and water as David Garver (Eastwood) barrels preposterously down California's coastal Highway 1 to the sound of ersatz jazz-rock; or takes long walks with estranged girlfriend Tobie

(Donna Mills) by the ocean, along the beach, over the hills, into the woods – at one point a conversation with Tobie on a town sidewalk jumps incongruently to a location several miles away. The lovers are often filmed from such a long distance we can't always be sure it's them. A cheesy highlight of the movie is a naked waterfall-in-Eden love scene set to the sound of Roberta Flack singing "First Time Ever I Saw Your Face" – it's a long song – five minutes. Monterey, California must have chipped in some money as well: there's a clip from the Monterey Jazz Festival with music from the Johnny Otis Show (featuring the young Shuggie Otis in the background showcasing a cinema-worthy afro) and a shorter clip of Cannonball Adderley.

Eastwood's Garver is a radio DJ spinning soft jazz and reading sensuous poetry over the airwaves late at night. A woman named Evelyn (Jessica Walter) calls the station and makes repeated requests for Garver to "play '*Misty*,' for me." Banter between Garver and his black DJ friend Jay Jay (Duke Everts) lets us know that Garver has a problem keeping his dick in his pants – a retort to Garver's request for advice on his soured relationship with Tobie is met with "live by the sword, die by the sword."

Garver and Evelyn have a sexual tryst. What is casual sex for Garver is deadly infatuation for Evelyn. When Garver tries to dump her, Evelyn begins turning up unexpectedly, interrupting Garver at work, ruining a business meeting, attempting suicide in his bathroom, wrecking his house, stabbing his black maid, ultimately stabbing Garver after putting Tobie in bondage. Along the way, Garver calls in Detective Sgt. McCallum (John Larch) who, in neatly done Hitchcockian manner, meets an untimely dispatch.

Jessica Walter's crazed righteousness and banshee energy keeps Eastwood off balance as an actor. Responding to her psychotic outbursts, the actor's usual awkwardness and inarticulateness makes for a flustered performance that is

101

useful to this particular film. In retrospect, it's refreshing to see Eastwood in a casual mode, dressed down and looking as human as the rest of us. These roles are few, but I have a sporadic affection for Clint the dunderhead, the dumb guy who is in over his head.

The film was a box office success and launched Eastwood's directing career on sure footing. Andrew Sarris and Roger Ebert praised the film. Ebert pointed out rather obviously: "it is not the artistic equal of *Psycho*."

Breezy – 1973

At a time when his peers were exploding with films like *French Connection* and *The Exorcist* (Friedkin), *The Godfather* (Coppola), *American Graffiti* (Lucas), *Badlands* (Terrence Malick), *The Last Detail* (Hal Ashby), *Long Goodbye* and *California Split* (Altman), *Mean Streets* (Scorsese), *Last Picture Show* and *Paper Moon* (Bogdanovich), *Bananas* and *Sleepers* (Woody Allen), Eastwood somehow got stuck on his third film with a tepid drama called *Breezy*.

Breezy was an unusual entry in the director's early career. Eastwood isn't in the film and it isn't an action flick. The actors aren't shooting guns or holding up banks. The main character is a woman and she gets some screen time.

Kay Lenz is Breezy, a free-spirited hippie teenager running away from the overly strict home environment she found herself in after the death of her parents. Trying to escape the clutches of a predator who has picked her up hitchhiking, she ends up on the doorstep of a man well above her in age - Frank Harmon - played by William Holden. In seventies movie terms, "free-spirit" meant "casual sex." Frank and Breezy end up in bed. An emotional bond is formed when Frank begins to admire Breezy's honesty and loyalty.

Holden knows how to get comfortable in a role. Franks's life-fatigue seems genuine; gravity is pulling him down. Various quantities of alcohol are consumed. He's obviously depressed by his state of affairs, his ex-wife, his mortality.

Breezy flits about happily. Franks's spirits are lifted. He's had enough of cynicism. There isn't much drama. Breezy and Frank feel different sorts of pressure from their respective peer groups. One senses a little of Eastwood's sourness in the hippie scenes. These youngsters are dumb and / or manipulative - one beats his girlfriend and the rest are stoned, guitar-strumming druggies. There is some balance to this; Frank's old friends and business colleges are oppressive in their own way. They are repulsed by Breezy and skeptical about the age difference. Frank, feeling a sense of guilt, breaks up with Breezy, but eventually love prevails.

The film was shelved for a year by *Universal* and was a step back for Eastwood at the box office.

Firefox – 1982

The Russians have developed a new jet fighter that evades radar making it virtually invisible. Better than that, the aircraft's weaponry can be controlled through a pilot's "mind prompts" increasing the speed and efficiency of battle commands.

Mitchell Gant (Clint Eastwood) is an ex-fighter pilot who was shot down in Vietnam and captured by the enemy. During his rescue he saw a young Vietnamese girl consumed in a conflagration. His resulting PTSD, which is referred to here as "delayed response," has forced him to seek solitude in the Alaskan wilderness. In an example of how ideas about PTSD have dated – at one point when the subject of Gant's illness is brought up an army official remarks – "it isn't active when fighting, only at home." It doesn't matter, the PTSD won't have any impact on the plot.

Gant happens to be "the best pilot in the world." Tracked down in Alaska he is coerced into becoming part of a spy mission that will attempt to infiltrate Russia and hijack the super fighter jet.

The movie should be moderately appealing to spy fans. There are a few interesting twists and turns as Gant meets the spy network. He's forced into several identity changes; there's some nice cat and mouse at a Moscow transit terminal. Notes of realism and balderdash exist arm in arm, but in general Gant's progress into Russia and the proximity of the jet is way too easy to take seriously.

When Gant climbs into the cockpit of the plane and heads for freedom land, Russian pilots are in pursuit in their own super planes. This last half-hour of the film is weighted down with dull cross-cutting between Gant and American headquarters, and Russian pilots and Russian headquarters. The movie fizzles out as a video-game style dogfight unfolds between Gant and his Russian counterpart.

Bridges of Madison County – 1995

Bridges of Madison County is a *Harlequin* romance. Robert Kincaid (Eastwood), a *National Geographic* photographer who has traveled the world, finds himself in rural Iowa shooting a photo documentary on the county's quaint covered bridges. He meets Francesca Johnson (Meryl Steep), a farmer's wife who has been left alone when her husband, son and daughter drive a prize cow to the state fair. The timeframe is supposed to be 1965 but the film is so devoid of period details other than the antique-store décor at the farm house that it could just as well be the 1930s or the 1990s.

Francesca expresses vague disenchantment with Iowa and her family life. Robert suggests he has a girl in every port; but for a reason that is hard to fathom, he is smitten with Francesca. Eastwood is not very convincing expressing travel lust; and Meryl's character never gets desperate enough to suggest there is something really profound at stake – the movie could have used a little more angst, a little more humiliation. The film takes its time moving from sexual reticence to consummation. We witness a couple of dark nights and suggestions of skin, but the result is a cold affair.

The stilted mark of Steven Spielberg is present in the beginning and ending framing: Francesca's grown-up son and daughter, after her death, discover a diary that reveals the old love affair – these sequences are padded out, intended to suggest a bigger family mystery, but the deliberations are based on extremely banal events.

Film critic Janet Maslin noted the movie had "surprising decency." Certainly, she meant: "coming from Clint Eastwood."

You could find more convincing and compelling romances in any number of action / drama / comedies of the day consummated in half the screen time allowed here including *Before Sunrise*, *Don Juan DeMarco*, *French Kiss*, *To Die For*, *Leaving Las Vegas*, and *Sense and Sensibility*.

Blood Work – 2002

The movie begins with crime scene investigator Terry McCaleb (Eastwood) arriving in the aftermath of a serial killer's bloody rampage. We quickly learn that McCaleb has become entangled in a relationship with the killer who baits him with clues at the scene of each crime, taunting him and making him the subject of media attention. As McCaleb leaves the apartment where the murder has occurred, newsmen crowd around him, yelling out absurd questions in step-away-from-movie-extra voices. McCaleb notices a pair of bloody tennis shoe tracks and begins a pursuit of the suspect with nobody else caring to follow. McCaleb manages to find and wound the suspect, but he gets away. The physical effort gives McCaleb a massive heart attack which will require a heart transplant. The heart transplant will come from a murder victim.

MaCaleb retires and lives on a houseboat. Graciella Rivers (Wanda De Jesus), the sister of the murdered girl whose heart McCaleb is now carrying, contacts him and asks him to try to find her sister's killer. McCaleb feels obligated. He and his neighbor Buddy Noone (Jeff Daniels) begin investigating.

I don't know why it's easy to peg Jeff Daniels as the serial killer from the moment you see him. Maybe it's because he is so unlike a serial killer. Also, no one else shows up that begs consideration. There is a labored attempt to set up a mysterious horror subtext regarding McCaleb's doctor Bonnie Fox (Angelica Huston) and her role in the heart transplant. Meanwhile, Buddy, the serial killer, misses his notoriety. He kidnaps Graciella and McCaleb saves her. Graciella and McCaleb live happily ever after on the houseboat. It's a tired exercise in suspense.

Mystic River – 2003

In the opening scenes on a Boston city street, three adolescent boys – Jimmy, Sean and Dave – are engaged in a mild act of vandalism (writing their names in wet cement) when a man posing as law enforcement flashes a badge and begins to harass them. His interaction with the kids is protracted, but nobody in the neighborhood notices – the streets are strangely empty. The man coerces Dave into his car and sprints him away as Jimmy and Sean watch helplessly. The victim, Dave, is held captive and sexually abused but manages to escape. When the police return him to his parents, a neighbor is overheard saying: "He's damaged goods."

Flash ahead several years and the three kids have grown up. Jimmy Markum (Sean Penn) owns a store and has a wife, Annabeth (Laura Linney), a 19-year-old daughter from a previous marriage named Katie (Emmy Rossum), and two younger girls. Sean Devine (Kevin Bacon) is a homicide detective; his wife has left him. The abducted kid, Dave Boyle (Tim Robbins) is still traumatized by his experience; he is married to Celeste (Marcia Gay Harden) and has a young son named Michael (Cayden Boyd).

One night, a car belonging to Jimmy's daughter is found bloodied and abandoned. Katie's body will be discovered in the nearby woods bludgeoned and twice shot. Katie's boyfriend Brendon Harris (Tom Guiry) becomes the prime suspect when Detective Devine and his partner

Whitey Powers (Lawrence Fishburne) find out the couple had been planning to run away to Las Vegas to get married. On the same night of the murder, in what will be one of a few-too-many coincidences in *Mystic River*, Dave stumbles into his house, his stomach slashed and bleeding, blood on his clothes. He tells Celeste of an attempted mugging – that he fought back, pounded the assailant's head into the pavement – he may have killed him. She consoles him and they keep it secret.

Feverish acting ensues on the part of Penn, Robbins and Harden. Penn's Jimmy is grounded most securely in the parameters of a full-blown character. Penn hits perfect marks in scenes at a younger daughter's communion, at the scene of the crime, at the morgue, and at the wake. Our initial compassion toward Jimmy begins to wane as we learn more about him: he's an ex-con who has been involved in armed robberies. Jimmy was ratted out by Ray Harris, the deceased father of Brendon Harris, and as a result Jimmy spent time in jail. We learn that Jimmy murdered Ray Harris after his incarceration. Although Jimmy has been straight for years, he still associates with criminals like the Savage brothers (Kevin Chapman and Adam Nelson).

Marsha Gay Harden as Dave's wife Celeste is nervous and harried; you don't know if she needs acting guidance or meds. She enters the movie fretting and leaves the movie fretting.

Tim Robbin's character, Dave, is a giant walking false crime lead with a big "red herring" sign hanging around his neck. The audience is supposed to be somewhat open to the idea that Dave killed Katie – and Eastwood pushes the point so hard Dave can't react like a normal human being. *Mystic River* is one of those films Roger Ebert complained about: if a main character would just disclose a bit of information, or explain to somebody what actually happened, and defend themselves against growing suspicions, the whole film would be relieved of the ensuing tragedy. Instead, Dave, who at times seems perfectly reasonable, becomes opaque and uncommunicative at the wrong moments. At one point he stares at a horror flick playing on the television and rants about vampires. When Celeste tells Jimmy she's become afraid of Dave and has moved out – Jimmy later recounts to Dave "Celeste told me she thinks you murdered Katie." A statement that comes from nowhere.

Bacon's Detective Devine fares the worst and reminds us that Eastwood isn't very attentive to performance. Some of Bacon's line readings are like edits from a dress rehearsal.

There are a couple of melodramatic "God's-Eye-View" camera shots that Eastwood had become fond of during this phase of his career. Every once in a while, ecclesiastical music (by Eastwood) bursts in to remind us this is a serious story with maybe something important to say about life. Eastwood was writing his own soundtracks and the results had become increasingly distracting.

As a murder mystery, *Mystic River* is frustrating. Early on, we hear a 911 call in which a young kid's voice reports Katie's abandoned car. The 911 dispatcher asks, "What's your name?" The kid hears this wrong and replies to somebody who is with him: "They want to know *her* name." The dispatcher repeats "What's *your* name?" And the kid's voice replies: "We're outta here." Second guessers in the audience may realize the significance right away. The detectives aren't so smart. Much later in the film, Katie's boyfriend Brendon has passed a polygraph text. Detective Devine and Whitey are out of leads. Devine pulls a cassette recording of the original 911 call and asks Whitey: "Was there anything on the 911 call?" Whitey replies: "I thought you listened to it." Sean says: "I thought you listened to it." They play the tape and Whitey hears nothing, but Sean says, "Listen." In other words, how did the kid know it was a "she" if the body wasn't in the car (a more pertinent question might be: why did they bother calling 911 anyway since they end up being the murderers?).

Meanwhile, coincidences pile up: the gun used in Katie's murder is traced back to Brendan's murdered father Ray Harris. Why was Katie murdered? Brendon's mute younger brother, Silent Ray, along with a friend, just happened to show up at the location where Katie just happened to be. They just happened to be playing with a gun which went off accidentally and hit her, and since they are the kind of young kids who don't want her to tell anybody, they chase her into the woods, hit her and shoot her again. (I'm not sure Silent Ray's friend is ever given a name in the film, and while watching the film I thought he might be another brother of Brendon's.) And it happens at that exact point where the detectives are finally listening to the 911 call, Jimmy and the Savage brothers have picked up Dave, forced him into a false confession and killed him.

The film has trouble winding down. There's a nice scene with Detective Devine telling a drunken Jimmy that Dave has disappeared. There's a bizarre scene – Laura Linney's only extended one as Jimmy's wife – where she coaxes him into better spirits by horridly disparaging Dave. Later, the families are all gathered at a Boston parade. Dave's wife Celeste is still running around frantically as Detective Devine and Jimmy exchange perplexing hand signals to each other – like they belong to some mysterious rite.

Is *Mystic River* finally an Eastwood rumination on the vigilante theme – how taking the law into your own hands might not be a good thing? Penn's Jimmy seems pretty disgusting after all is said and done. But Dave took the law into his own hands as well: he wasn't mugged like he told Celeste; he accosted a child molester in action and murdered him. *Mystic River* suggests a world of perennial victims and

114

misguided, violent brutes. It's a Godless world despite the genuflections that are thrown about. It's a hard film to watch – relentlessly grim.

Letters from Iwo Jima – 2006

Letters from Iwo Jima, a companion piece to *Flags of Our Fathers,* tells the story of the attack on Iwo Jima from the point of view of the Japanese defending the island.

As the Japanese prepare for the invasion, digging holes on the beach and disguising caves and bunkers filled with weapons and ammunition, a new commander arrives. General Kuribayashi (Ken Watanabe) is secretly privy to disastrous battles that have left the Japanese naval fleet in ruins and he quickly recognizes the futility of the upcoming defense of the island. General Kuribayashi is given a back-story: a Japanese diplomat to the USA before the war, he still carries around the *Colt 45* given to him as a present by an American delegation on one of his visits. He is happy to find a familiar face on the island who represents the larger world: Baron Nishi (Tsuyoshi Ihara), an Olympic medalist who has traveled far and wide as a celebrity.

It is the foot soldier Saigo (Kazynari Ninomiya) whom we follow for most of the film. He is a chronic complainer, skeptical about the war and the officers in charge. In a culture that (here at least) is ready to fight to their last dying breath or commit suicide to avoid being captured, Saigo has the anti-authoritarian genetic makeup that includes a huge dose of self-preservation. As in *Slaughterhouse Five,* Saigo lunges clumsily from disaster to disaster. Often weaponless, he comes out mostly unscratched as fellow soldiers meet gruesome deaths all around him. His comrades include Kashawara (Takashi Yamaguchi) who will die of dysentery and Private Shimizu (Ryo Kase) who is murdered after surrendering to American troops.

Spread out in caves around the island, water and food are scarce. The Americans arrive, first in a wave of aerial bombing, second as a huge naval force. Almost immediately communications are destroyed between the Japanese held caves and panic ensues. General Kuribayashi orders a retreat from some of the caves, but a dissenting commander orders his men to commit suicide, and for the most part they comply – pulling pins from grenades and smacking them on their helmets, they blow themselves to pieces one by one. Not Saigo – he runs when he gets a chance.

As things fall apart, Baron Nishi leads a frontal battle on the Americans but most of his men are killed and Nishi is blinded – after ordering his men to join troops elsewhere, he kills himself with a rifle.

Saigo manages to rejoin General Kuribayashi and is led again into a head-on battle where most of the men are killed. The General is mortally wounded. Before he dies, he asks Saigo to bury him. Saigo is doing so when captured by American troops. He attempts to fight them but is knocked unconscious. He wakes up lying on the beach alongside a great many wounded American soldiers awaiting transport home.

The time frame seems like a few days, though the battle for Iwo Jima lasted almost a month, and little interest is given to the expanse of the battle.

The characters also seem truncated and ideas about war, from the Japanese perspective, are barely thought out. The Japanese soldiers aren't well-etched despite the fact that a few get short, sentimentalized back stories. The sensitive aristocratic men of the world – Baron Nishi and General Kuribayashi – display some affection for their troops. They are cast against the more brutal officers who are ready to behead, beat, disparage. Then there are the grunts – just following orders. An act of mercy on a wounded American soldier by the Japanese has a counterpart in a war crime enacted on a surrendering Japanese soldier by an American soldier – sort of a PBS stew of all ideas equalized. Any insights into a war of aggression gone extremely wrong is ignored in favor of an Americanized idea of war psyche; mass suicide excluded. They might as well be American soldiers. The screenwriters – mostly Paul Haggis – are looking at the characters from the outside, writing with little eye for larger themes and larger intentions – a "war-is-hell-for-everybody" attitude is the best he can offer. "Cultural assistance" was provided by Iris Yamashita (Yamashita was born in Missouri but is said to have experience with "Japanese culture").

The overall effect is of Eastwood trying to pull off a prestige picture coup by filming two war movies at once. This is as artsy as he gets. Audiences didn't turn out in numbers large enough to pull either film high into *Academy Award* territory (*Letters from Iwo Jim*a garnered Alan Robert Murray and Bub Asman an award for Best Sound Editing).

Changeling – 2008

Like many films that have started with the introduction "a true story," *Changeling* doesn't feel like it contains an ounce of truth.

Eastwood has often used cinematography that dulls down the universe, but there was an acceleration of the process around *Flags of Our Fathers* that devolved into the colorless palette of *Changeling*. Browns, denuded blues, pale soft colors seem to be hiding problems with the 1928 time-frame of the film. The street scenes in particular are blurry. Added to this is the moribund nature of the set designs – house, police station, jury room, farm – the intermittently tacky, miserly nature of Eastwood's productions were reaching new lows around this point.

The problems extend to the acting as well. Angelina Jolie, John Malkovich, Michael Kelly and Jeffrey Donovan (particularly Jeffrey Donovan) speak so stiffly it makes you uncomfortable. The actors look puzzled about their characters – like the film isn't making any more sense to them than it is to the audience. For several scenes, Jolie sticks to a deadpan expression that is void of context; your eyes keep drifting to her bright red lipstick because there is nothing else to watch. Other times, Jolie clutches her head with anguished pain and you see her wig move to the right or the left ever so slightly. She's bundled up and swathed in clothes that blare "antique." The actors throw their lines at each other; they seem to be launching wild modulations into

119

large empty spaces. Whatever happened in the "true" story certainly had nothing to do with the unbelievable mess offered here.

It's 1928, Los Angeles. Christine Collins (Jolie) is unexpectedly called into work on her day off. She reluctantly leaves her young son Walter (Gattlin Griffith) at home alone, but promises to be back by four. She arrives home late and Walter is missing. Frantic, she searches the neighborhood (something fishy in the way there are obviously houses around but not many neighbors and Christine is never shown spreading the word about her lost son). She calls the police but they tell her most kids show up within 24 hours so they can't do anything. She is alarmed but doesn't protest successfully and is forced to wait. In the morning a cop car shows up. A search begins.

Meanwhile, the Los Angeles Police Department is festering with corruption. The Reverend Gustav Briegleb (Malkovich) gives regular radio sermons on police graft and violence. The subplot is half-written – Briegleb's crusade, despite his large congregation, has little effect on anything taking place in the film.

Weeks pass by. Christine holds out hope and is still searching for her son in her own way, but nothing is turning up. Finally, the LAPD contact her and tell her they've found Walter in Dekalb, Illinois. She meets Captain J.J. Jones (Donovan) who is immediately shown to be an uncaring asshole hoping for some good PR and a photo op for the LAPD. Jones speaks in creepy sentences that expose him as a complete slime ball – nobody would ever believe a single word from this guy. When the train arrives that should have Walter on board, Christine and Jones are there to greet him along with a group of newspaper reporters. Lo and behold, when the kid gets off the train, it isn't Walter.

Christine quietly protests that the boy is not her son. Jones treats this with skepticism. The reporters stand about

120

like extras – not allowed to chime in (the scene seems to have been filmed simultaneously with the train scene at the end of the film where the newsmen extras will be dressed exactly the same). Jones tells Christine she's crazy – the kid is Walter, maybe he changed in five weeks, she's not straight in her mind, just take the boy please. She continues to protest, and he convinces her to take the kid (you know – like maybe try him out for a bit) and she somehow says okay, maybe they can keep looking for Walter if she takes the kid.

The audience probably expects Christine to take the kid home and start telling everybody – teachers, postmen, neighbors, newspapers or even one single friend – look, it's not Walter, the police screwed up. (Wouldn't somebody else notice?) Instead, everybody in town stays invisible, this is the loneliest, most isolated woman that looks like Angelina Jolie that anyone has ever encountered. Whatever isolation the original Christine Collins dealt with is not given a believable facsimile. Ignorance, ugliness, even some kind of collusion with the police might have played a part in the scenario. Absolutely no time is spent on the elephant in the room: Christine's relationship with the kid who knows he isn't her son.

Instead, Christine continues to cooperate with the police until Captain J.J. Jones finally just tells her she's nuts – the kid is Walter and he doesn't want to hear anything more about it. The way this is played, it's hard to tell if Jones knows it isn't Walter or thinks it might be Walter or just doesn't care one way or the other and doesn't understand how this might have a downside. Later we learn they have a picture of Walter in the police files – anybody could have checked it out – and of course Christine could have just shown them a photo.

Christine begins letting the secret out. Walter's dentist and his school teacher write statements saying it isn't Walter.

The Reverend Briegleb picks up on Christine's problems and joins her in exposing the LAPD mistake.

The LAPD sends a psychiatrist to Christine's house and he tells her that Walter has just shrunk a few inches due to trauma. She disagrees. The interview gets her committed to an asylum thanks to a sign-off by the LAPD.

At the asylum, Christine finds out that women are being incarcerated by order of the police department. One woman was beaten by a police officer and when she tried to report the crime, she was thrown into the asylum. At this point, the treatment of women in 1928 becomes a focus of the film for a short time. Later, as Christine's story becomes better known, this subplot will loosely be tied in to scenes of street protests and legal action in favor of women's rights. The heroic aspects written into the script seem to be actions taken by lawyers who barely show up in the movie.

Meanwhile, another LAPD detective, Lester Ybarra (Michael Kelly), is sent out to a farm house to pick up a kid (Eddie Alderson) who has snuck into the USA from Canada. When Ybarra takes the boy back to the police station, he confesses that his Uncle Gordon Northcott (Jason Harner), who lives at the farm, has killed 20 kids with an ax. He also identifies Walter as one of the kids who was at the farm. The kid's flashbacks are disturbingly gruesome and add another layer to the film – this one completely sensationalized in an unwatchable manner.

The LAPD is forced to admit its mistake. There is a community uproar. The murderer Northcott manages to escape. Canadian police capture him and he is returned to Los Angeles. The murder trial and a LAPD civil lawsuit seem to take place simultaneously. Northcott is found guilty and sentenced to death. The LAPD is no longer able to commit women to the asylum. A few people are fired.

When the execution is scheduled, the murderer invites Christine to see him and promises her he will tell her about the fate of Walter. She goes, but he ends up not telling her. She witnesses his hanging – the hanging is staged "realistically" – but Christine is so deadpan you don't even know if she cares.

Christine holds out hope that Walter is alive as the movie ends.

J. Edgar – 2011

J. Edgar is shot in half-light, paced by a score (courtesy of Eastwood) that tinkles bell tones to introduce a few too many somber scenes, and told in swift flashbacks as FBI Director J. Edgar Hoover (Leonardo DiCaprio) nearing the end of his career recalls the events that transformed the organization. Screenwriter Dustin Lance Black spends quality time on the repressed sexuality and secret love between Hoover and his Deputy Director Clyde Tolson (Armie Hammer). The story races through the highlights of FBI history including the Communist menace, gangsters, and the Lindbergh kidnapping. Adding uneasily to the back-and-forth nature of the film are subplots involving Hoover falsifying the events in which he has been most notoriously involved as he dictates his memoirs, at the same time he is spying on Martin Luther King, Jr. and sparring with Richard Nixon. The film never finds a consistent narrative rhythm and lacks epic cinematic proportion – it's a small film pretending to be a big film. In a few places (in particular the Lindbergh sequences) the storyline gets short-changed. The heart of the story is the homosexuality, though the actors arrive in old-face make-up much too soon (poor Armie looks like a mummy). A better film might have dwelt further on these issues especially if offered with irony and some sexual-historical context (i.e., what screenwriter Black did with the movie *Harvey Milk* and the television series *Big Love*).

As Edgar's mother Annie, Judy Dench avoids Hitchcockian overtones even as she swamps Edgar with manipulative feedback and self-interested ambition. The film reaches a psychological highpoint when Edgar and Clyde are out on the town but stuck at a table with a group of ladies: Edgar relates gangbusters stories even as the women size them up and start teasing them. When one of women asks Edgar to dance, panic ensues and the duo flees. Edgar returns home and tells his mother what happened. Annie, after giving Edgar a lecture on the dangers of being a "daffodil," teaches him to dance. One senses where the screenwriter's heart lies.

DiCaprio is alternately bullish and desperately vulnerable, hiding self-realization behind a veneer of resolved turpitude and clumsy force. Naomi Watts plays Hoover's loyal secretary Helen Gandy, but is restricted to smiles and frowns and short lines. The rest of the cast flies by for quick scenes or sequences, none very effective.

Jersey Boys – 2014

It's possible Clint Eastwood's interest in *Jersey Boys* was nothing more than the chance to put a Broadway musical (in this case a "jukebox musical" – not the same thing) under his belt. The plot is a memoir-style biography of the band The Four Seasons. The movie could have been about The Young Rascals, Tommy James and the Shondells, Vanilla Fudge or any number of young music groups from the fifties and sixties; the details are somewhat interchangeable. The musical numbers are truncated – kind of losing the point of making a movie about The Four Seasons in the first place. Eastwood doesn't offer any deep cuts from the band – most were hit singles. The result is like watching an oldies music show interspersed with band arguments. The criminal activity displayed by the young band members in the early scenes and the band's interaction with Mafia crime families never take on any emotional gravity. Where is Ken Russell when you need him?

These Jersey boys dress a lot better and dance a lot better than The Four Seasons ever did in their many appearances on sixties television. The Frankie Valli in *Jersey Boys (*John Lloyd Young) starts out sounding like Jerry Lewis but eventually settles into a falsetto that shows the craftiness of the original melodies. It's funny how films like this are never about the creative process. I cringed every time songwriter Bob Guadio (Erich Bergan) sat down at the piano and offered up a new song which the boys executed perfectly in four-part harmony on the first run through. The third act is foreshadowed with suggestions of an upcoming magnum opus, but settles on the clattery, over- produced pop throwback of "Can't Take My Eyes Off of You."

The last scene is the most rousing – the entire cast doing a splashy choreographed Broadway version of "December 1963 (Oh, What a Night)" – a song I never liked, but which works well here.

Do yourself a favor. Go back and check out the records – the music is warmer, fuzzier and maybe sloppier, but you'll find a lot of good songs by The Four Seasons that you may have never heard before.

Jersey Boys was a box office flop.

Sully – 2016

Sully has the offhand feel of a low-budget docu-drama created for some obscure cable station. It's an it-really-happened pic focusing on Captain Sullenberger's landing of a *US Airways* passenger airplane in the middle of the Hudson River in January of 2009. Since it was "torn from today's headline" you may feel like you've already seen it. Other than the actual landing on the water and the exit of the passengers from the plane, the movie is a fairly boring procedural about the investigation by *US Airways* that followed the crash, and Sully's subsequent feelings regarding the event.

Tom Hanks plays Sully with an arms-crossed "don't bother me" expression on his face. Like Eastwood, he fails to locate any real anti-authoritarian anger or post-accident trauma – because little seems to have existed. Thankfully the film is brief and it's probably worth knowing the mechanics of landing a gigantic airliner on top of a busy waterway.

The 15:17 to Paris – 2018

Six of Eastwood last ten films had been biographical or based-on-actual-event stories. With the exception of a few story-telling elements in *J. Edgar* and the box office power of *American Sniper*, the genre was not very successful for Eastwood. As with the airplane sequence in *Sully*, the only cinematically interesting aspect of *The 15:17 to Paris* is the event that inspired the movie, namely the solo terrorist attack thwarted by three Americans on board an Amsterdam to Paris train in 2015. The incident earns about 15 minutes of screen time.

It was a mistake to base the film on the biographical background of three ordinary heroes who had been friends since childhood. There is little drama anywhere as they move from non-distinct school chums, to clumsy adolescents, to not particularly inspiring American men. Eastwood allowed the three heroes to play themselves in the movie and they never find a comfortable rhythm with the ever-present small talk. The result is tedious and you may end up resenting the tourist advertisements for Italy, Germany and Amsterdam intertwined with commercials for *Coke*, *Instagram* and selfie-sticks (other commercials include a young kid prominently showing off his gun collection which includes a toy MG, a toy AK and a real hunting rifle).

Lesser

Cinematic

Foolishness

Lesser Cinematic Foolishness

Bronco Billy – 1980

Ringmaster Doc Lynch (Scatman Crothers), rope-master Leonard James (Sam Bottoms), snake dancer Chief Big Eagle (Dan Vadis) and his helper Running Water (Sierra Pecheur), and driver Lefty Lebow (Bill McKinney) are the lesser attractions in a struggling Wild West cowboy show that features the sharp-shooter and horse trickster Bronco Billy (Eastwood).

The movie starts with the tropes of a screwball comedy: an obnoxious New York society girl – Antoinette Lilly (Sandra Locke) – has to be married in order to receive the family fortune. In ostentatious fashion, Antoinette sports a long cigarette holder and walks around with her nose up in the air as she spouts affected English (you almost expect her to shove a monocle into one eye). She decides to marry a flunky by the name of John Arlington (Geoffrey Lewis) who is smarter than he looks and plans to rip her off. When Arlington leaves her high and dry in a southwest motel, she runs into Bronco Billy who offers her work with the crew and / or a ride to the next town. Lilly is disgusted with the troupe. Locke's performance is stilted at first, but begins to settle in as it bounces off the squareness of Eastwood and his buddies.

Since the director / actor is too laconic for screwball comedy the movie eventually finds a slower, more familiar, Eastwoodian gait. A certain Americana expressiveness is revealed as Bronco Billy performs to the "little partners" and their parents who show up for the cowboy shows in varying numbers. Eastwood may have missed his forte playing lug-headed characters.

Bronco Billy's show does charity work for mental institutions and orphanages. As Antoinette meets Billy's friends, she begins to thaw a bit. This is accelerated when Billy rescues her during an attempted rape that follows one of those ridiculous Eastwood bar fights. Unfortunately, Billy's show tent burns down during a performance at the same time rope-artist Leonard is busted for being a Vietnam deserter. In an effort to save the show, Billy attempts to retrieve Leonard from jail. We already know Bronco Billy is a master gunman because earlier in the film during one of those stereotypical bank robbery scenes, Billy shoots the guns out of the robbers' hands and then uses the notoriety to plug the night's performance when the news crew arrives. As a result, Billy's confrontation with the sheriff who arrested Leonard comes off as bizarre. The sheriff wants to test Billy's gun fighting prowess and challenges him to a gunfight. He taunts Billy. Billy backs down, even admitting "I'm a coward." Eastwood is playing against type but there is something fishy about the editing of this scene; for one thing, it ends in suspense, and you don't actually know how the incident is resolved – he just shows up later with Leonard. It's almost like Eastwood was hedging how he wanted to showcase the cowardice part and maybe wasn't satisfied with the end result.

What lifts *Bronco Billy* above the usual Eastwood fare is the idea at the center of the screenplay: the cowboy performers are all fakers. Billy is an ex-shoe-salesmen. The others are ex-cons who served prison time together and recreated themselves under the tutelage of Bronco Billy.

Antoinette Lily ultimately gives in to the same kind of makeover. The film carries a buoyant sensitivity not usually found in an Eastwood film.

Eastwood made a perplexing statement about *Bronco Billy*: "… if, as a film director, I ever wanted to say something, you'll find it in *Bronco Billy*." But I don't buy it – Eastwood is no *Bronco Billy*.

Andrew Sarris listed *Bronco Billy* as one of his favorite films of the year alongside *Altered States* (Ken Russell), *American Gigolo* (Paul Schrader), *The Big Red One* (Sam Fuller), *Raging Bull* (Martin Scorsese), *The Shining* (Stanley Kubrick) and *Wise Blood* (John Huston). The movie doesn't really have the gravity of those films – technically, emotionally or aesthetically, but it is hard to fault on a small scale.

A Perfect World - 1993

Two convicts break out of prison in Texas, kidnap a prison worker, murder him, then break into a house and kidnap a young child in the presence of his mother. Terry Pugh (Keith Szarabajka) is a cold-blooded murderer. Butch Haynes (Kevin Costner) is a career criminal - a burglar, armed robber, and at the age of 8 killed a man who was brutalizing his mother at the brothel where he was raised. Phillip Perry a.k.a. Buzz (T.J. Lowther) is the kidnapped boy raised as a Jehovah's Witness with his mother Gladys (Jennifer Griffin) and two sisters.

As a Jehovah's Witness, Phillip has been deprived of the usual childhood rites of passage - like Halloween, Christmas, carnivals. At first, Butch manipulates Phillip, but a bond begins to form between them. When Terry attempts to abuse Phillip, Butch kills Terry and leaves him in a cornfield.

Hot on the trail is Texas Ranger Red Garnett (Eastwood), a criminal psychologist named Sally (Laura Dern), FBI agent Bobby Lee (Bradley Whitford), and a slew of police and rangers. Red is carrying a load of guilt regarding Butch. When Butch was a juvenile and caught for a crime, Red convinced a judge to give him a longer than usual sentence. His explanation: Butch's father was an abusive, violent person and Butch would be better off in prison. The long sentence turned Butch into a hardened ex-con.

Eastwood's Red is fairly subdued and most of the story revolves around Butch and Phillip as they maneuver their way through the backwoods and farm roads of Texas heading for

136

Amarillo. The car chase scene involves a pickup towing a large criminologist's trailer and is short and sweet. Eastwood's auteur status is never more palpable than in the horrible scene where another of his lascivious waitresses invites Butch for a tryst while Phillip watches. Laura Dern is wasted in her few female vs male "comedy" exchanges.

Given the themes here - the bonding between a violent criminal and an innocent child - a more than usual amount of delicacy is required. Butch builds his rapport with Phillip by extolling the size of Phillip's penis, letting him ride on top of his car, exhorting him to rebel against his mother's religious restrictions (Phillip steals a Halloween costume at a store), and allows the boy to play with guns.

The depiction of post-traumatic stress disorder may make the film an uncomfortable viewing experience for some people. Phillip and his family had been subjected to a violent home invasion by Terry and Butch. Pistols and shotguns had been held to heads and brandished about. His mother beaten, Phillip was slugged in the jaw and knocked to the floor. During the subsequent escape, Terry starts to get reckless. Butch forces Phillip to hold a gun on Terry. Terry physically attacks the boy and chases him into a field, but before he can catch Phillip, Terry is shot by Butch. Butch steals a car from a farm house. The farmer jumps and grabs the passenger side of the window. Butch pulls his gun, intent on shooting him in the face. Phillip bites the farmer's hand and he goes tumbling into a ditch. When Butch and Phillip pick up a ride with a family on a road trip, at one point the mother starts harshly disciplining her kids and we see the triggering effect this has on Butch - it becomes uncertain where this is going to lead. Butch abandons the family at the side of the road and takes their car.

The psychological ramifications are muddled when repeated later. An African-American farmer finds Butch and Phillip asleep in his cornfield and in a friendly manner invites them to his home for a meal. They meet the farmer's mother and the farmer's son who is about Phillip's age. At first, they all get along, but when the father starts beating the boy, Butch is triggered to violence. He beats the father mercilessly, tapes him up while threatening him with a gun. When he begins duct-taping the family and binding them with rope, Phillip's own trauma begins to show up. Growing fearful of Butch's intentions, Phillip takes the gun, shoots Butch in the gut and runs away.

The screenwriter - John Lee Hancock - is trying to mirror the idea of Butch's original innocence with the actions of Phillip, but it's much too heavy of a pull. The soundtrack treats some of the duo's exploits as bluegrass comedy running down the road in funny escapade manner - like an unmoored *Bonnie and Clyde* or a drunken *Thieves Like Us* that doesn't have its ideas of violence thoroughly meted. Other times the soundtrack is trying to give the characters an elegiac humanism that is never really earned. Butch is vile. The kid is a mess. When Butch catches up to Phillip after Phillip shoots him, Butch suggests that he didn't intend to hurt the farm family and confesses "I only killed two people - one was hurting my mother, one who was hurting you" - it's not believable because virtually everybody Butch has come across in the film has been terrorized, hurt, demoralized or corrupted (and it leaves out the prison worker killed at the start of the movie). Luckily, a mighty law enforcement entourage has tracked Butch and Phillip down. An FBI sharp-shooter will soon leave Butch dead in a field though he is unarmed and about to turn himself in.

Costner is quite good as Butch - half smarmy / half knowingly gracious - a con man through and through. The sentimentality in the last couple of scenes may bring a tear or two.

Absolute Power – 1997

As *Absolute Power* was winding down, I was wondering why it was more enjoyable than most Eastwood action films. The film's beginning credits were sparse and it wasn't until the end credits that I noticed William Goldman wrote the screenplay. Goldman's estimable career has included scripts for *Harper*, *Papillon*, *All the President's Men*, *A Bridge Too Far*, *Magic*, *Heat*, *Misery*, *Chaplin*, *Butch Cassidy and the Sundance Kid*, and *The Princess Bride*, among others. This explains the movie's soberness in tone and absence of pandering digressions.

The extended first sequence shows the hand of a writer who will not be rushed. Luther Whitney (Eastwood) is a master jewel thief. He stealthily breaks into the multi-storied mansion of rich philanthropist Walter Sullivan (E.G. Marshall). In an upstairs bedroom, Luther discovers a room hidden behind a huge mirror that holds a treasure trove of artwork, jewelry and cash. He pilfers as much as he can. He starts to make an exit but hears voices and approaching footsteps. He ducks back into the hidden room and encloses himself within.

The mirror is two-way. Luther watches as a well-dressed man and woman, stumbling and obviously drunk, enter the bedroom. As they banter, Luther realizes this is the philanthropist's wife Christy (Melora Hardin) and an illicit lover. Christy assures her guest that husband Walter is gone – she has pleaded sickness to avoid going to Barbados with him on a holiday. An inebriated sexual tryst begins, but the man starts to get rough. He slaps her. She gets mad and things escalate. He attempts to strangle her, but Christy grabs a letter opener. She stabs the man in the arm and straddles him. She is about to stab him again when two men burst through the bedroom door and shoot her dead.

They are quickly joined by a woman. They revive the man, and discuss a way to cover-up the murder. They spend several hours cleaning the room, washing the blood, hiding evidence – the whole time Luther is watching. The woman puts the bloodied letter opener into a plastic bag. As they prepare to leave, she accidentally drops the letter opener behind a short table.

Feeling safe, Luther comes out of hiding. He retrieves the letter opener and puts it in his bag. Outside, the woman notices the missing evidence. The two men rush back up the stairs and Luther barely gets out of a window in time. He leads the men on a chase through the woods, and though he escapes in his car they are able to get the license number.

Shortly thereafter the audience learns the violent man is Alan Richmond, the President of the United States of America (Gene Hackman). The two men who shadow him are secret service agents Bill Burton (Scott Glenn) and Tim Collin (Dennis Haysbert). The woman is Chief-of-Staff Gloria Russell (Judy Davis). The detective in charge of the murder investigation will be Seth Frank (Ed Harris).

Kate (Laura Linney) is Luther's estranged daughter. Luther had been incarcerated for larceny and during that time Kate's mother died. In the interim she has become an attorney. After the murder, Luther begins to contact her hoping for reconciliation. Seth, the detective, in tracking Luther, will become romantically attracted to Kate.

Walter Sullivan hires a hit man to track and kill Luther, and the pressure intensifies from all directions. It's all fairly enjoyable melodrama but hardly a personal or ambitious film. The ensemble is generally affecting. For his part, Eastwood is affable and relaxed. The romantic interplay between Laura Linney and Ed Harris is sober (it shows that "surprising decency" again).

David Baldacci wrote the book from which the screenplay was adapted.

Midnight in the Garden of Good and Evil - 1997

John Kelso (John Cusack), a New York writer, arrives in Savannah, Georgia to do a short society piece for *Town and Country* magazine about an upper-echelon Christmas party thrown yearly by a local antiques dealer and self-made millionaire named Jim Williams (Kevin Spacey). Jim is secretly gay and involved in a tempestuous relationship with white trash hustler Billy Hanson (Jude Law). Kelso, the writer, will slowly be introduced to the eccentric citizens of Savannah. These include Jim's loyal and expert lawyer, Sonny Seiler (Jack Thompson) who has a bulldog, Ugo IV, that happens to be the mascot of the Georgia Bulldogs; Betty Harty (Kim Hunter) an aged movie star from silent films who still flirts and preens; Minerva (Irma P. Hall), a voodoo empress, and Lady Chablis (played by Chablis Deveau) an African-American transsexual. Kelso will also meet Joe Odom (Paul Hipp) and Mandy Nicholls (Alison Eastwood) - a piano player / singer duo.

The film's running time is 2 hours, 35 minutes and it's a sprawling story. There are a lot of characters and everybody is treated with respect - the gay Williams, the transsexual Lady Chablis, the intellectual Yankee writer, Kelso, the steadfast lawyer Sonny and the opportunistic squatter / performer Joe Odom. When a relationship starts between the singer Mandy and the writer Kelso it takes time to develop. This joins the two other sensibly realistic romances Eastwood has managed to put on screen in *Bird* and *Absolute Power*. This is Eastwood's rainbow movie.

The Savannah, Georgia locales are luscious; the movie is filmed in architectural treasures including the Mercer House (once owned by songwriter Johnny Mercer) and the Comer House. The production design by Henry Bumstead and art direction by Jack Taylor is sensuously detailed. The costumes and southern airs have the right feel. The expertise here extends to longtime collaborators Joel Cox (editor) and Jack N. Green (cinematographer).

The film is based on John Berendt's best-selling non-fiction book of the same name. The screenplay is by John Lee Hancock. Fans of the book have generally groused at the elision of characters, the encapsulation of the court trial at the end of the movie (there are *four* trials in the book - would *anybody* sit through four trials at a movie???).

Also criticized was the screenwriter's idea to make the writer John Kelso more a part of the plot than he was in the book. Several critics including Roger Ebert found Kelso extraneous and felt the film would have been better without him. I can't imagine what would have happened without John Cusack as Kelso. Kelso leads us through the maze of Savannah's characters with a reporter's eye. Without his deft reaction shots to the various eccentricities, we might have had another cynical, misanthropic Eastwood flick, and a parade of grotesques. Cusack elevates the film's humanism, giving it a slant that is sometimes coy and hammy, but is pretty entertaining nonetheless.

At Kelso's first meeting with Jim Williams, he is taken by the southerner's dramatic drawl, sly wit and not-so-subtle flattery. They discuss art and art collecting. Kelso, when he doesn't have his notepad in hand, has acquired a habit of deep listening - you can almost see him writing and editing in his head as he talks to people. Jim and Kelso are both backslappers who can improvise when events get messy.

On Kelso's first night in Savannah, Megan the singer knocks on his door. She is looking for some ice for a party next door. She awakens Kelso and drags him out of bed. Her duet partner Joe Odom has taken over a friend's mansion while he is out of town. You can feel Kelso sizing up the huge house - given the sensory overload, his 500-word piece for the magazine will probably be a cinch.

The next night is the Christmas party. Jim introduces Kelso to the richer citizens of Savannah. Kelso snoops around a bit, and Jim invites him to look at some special art acquisitions. Billy Hanson bursts in and begins a heated argument with Jim about money. Billy leaves in a bad temper. Jim and Kelso discuss Billy. Kelso tells Jim he thinks he has enough material for his story and will be leaving in the morning.

Later that night, Kelso is awakened by noise. Outside, the police and an ambulance have taken over Jim's front yard. People from Joe Odom's party are milling about and they tell Kelso that Jim has shot Billy. A reporter's instinct kicks in. Kelso sneaks into the house and hears Jim's explanation of the shooting. The next morning Kelso calls his agent, tells him there's a bigger story in town and he wants to write a book.

The second act has a few problems. Kelso begins investigating and interviewing people Jim and Billy knew. Kelso meets the transsexual Lady Chablis, a friend of Billy's who can offer some evidence of his anger issues. Kelso and Chablis establish a bantering respect, Kelso's big-city seen-it-all inclusion, and Chablis' southern town cynicism fuse into friendship. Several sequences linked to the murder make sense - like a visit to the Women's Book Club of Savannah where people are gossiping about the shooting. There is one dud of a long scene at an African-American debutante's ball crashed by Lady Chablis where the Kelso-Chablis exchanges become redundant.

Jim invites Kelso to a graveyard at midnight to meet Minerva, the voodoo practitioner who is attempting to quell Billy's restless spirit and any affect it might be having on Jim

144

from beyond the grave. Eastwood usually uses spirituality and religion in a shallowly plotted manner, but these scenes are written more as a skeptical travelogue. Meanwhile, the Mandy and Kelso romance is off and on with reluctance by both parties bordering on disinterest. (Roger Ebert thought Kelso looked like he'd never been on a date, which misses the whole point of the slow burn - perhaps he expected another Eastwood quick-screw.)

A third act starts when Jim is arrested for murdering Billy. The Mandy and Kelso romance simmers, as Jim heads to trial. I can't really tell you still exactly what happened - Jim seems to be lying, but evidence is found that helps exonerate him.

I can't believe Eastwood's work here wasn't more encouraged by critics, but I guess they are not supposed to be his mentors. *Midnight in the Garden of Good and Evil* would open to mixed reviews and end up a dud at the box office. Predictably, what followed were safe formula conceits - *Blood Work* and *Space Cowboys*.

If the

Hundredth

Monkey

had Some Friends

If the Hundredth Monkey had Some Friends

Bird – 1988

Bird is a surprisingly good film biography based on the life of bebop-jazz giant Charlie Parker who died of a heart attack at the age of 34 after years of drug addiction, but managed in the forties to help point jazz in a new and unique direction.

What's different from most other Eastwood movies:

1. Eastwood doesn't take an acting role.

2. The script by Joel Oliansky isn't an infantile shoot-em-up – it's Eastwood's first real *drama* since *Breezy* back in 1973, and the first finessed script he's handled since *High Plains Drifter* (also in 1973).

3. The stars – Forrest Whitaker as Charlie Parker and Diane Venora as his girlfriend Chan – are perfectly cast.

4. The movie is longer than the usual Eastwood popcorn-selling venture, clocking in at 160 minutes which allows plenty of time for music as well as a poignant story-telling arc.

5. Eastwood's group of technicians are finally allowed to respond to something more than star vehicle machinery.

Bird shifts time-frames in a way that does great service to the three-pronged themes of drug / alcohol addiction, the general hardships of a musician's lifestyle, and the steadfastness of an odd beat-era love story. One minute Parker is clean and wailing his way through a classic performance, the next minute he's barely able to wheeze the last notes out for a recording session. There are times when he's flush in cash after a Jewish wedding, other times when he's desperate for money. In a love story never based on fealty, an overwhelming warmth of feeling is expressed that is strikingly original: Parker and Chan can almost mind-read each other; if their relationship appears doomed by Parker's predilections for drugs, they carry that weight with the perception of Parker's incredible gifts. Almost without speaking Chan makes Parker's struggles with self-disgust less self-destructive. Whitaker has a great mannerism in the film – the smile that is filled with pain.

The film doesn't let Parker off easy: to see Verona / Chan, legs crossed in an easy chair in a darkened apartment, listening to Whitaker / Parker jabbering in a roundabout manner that is both playful and anguished as he explains he's lost another job is as close to real life insight as Eastwood has put on screen. Even more chilling are the scenes where Parker has to interact with his three young children: he can be as childlike as they are, wallowing on the floor and giggling, but when one of them falls ill he is so avoidant he feels almost negligent – and you feel the load he puts on Chan.

The nocturnal ambiance of the film is one of its pleasures – late night bar scenes, pre-dawn love scenes, dull-lit recording studios, and crowded nighttime city streets capture the amped-up psyche of gigging musicians spilling over to fatigue or drunken bliss.

If we were to reassert a linear content to the film it would entail a couple of short scenes with Parker growing up, a short scene when he is warned at a very early age about his addiction, and a few scenes as he tries to assert his musical presence but doesn't have the skill, to his rather quick musical mastery, his romance with Chan, his friendship with Dizzy Gillespie (Samuel Wright), Red Rodney (Michael Zeiniker) and a few other jazz musicians, his womanizing, his struggle with addiction and his ultimate demise. The length of the film helps establish the reality of Parker's drug problems – shooting up, over-medicating himself with alcohol, kicking, complaining about problems like ulcers and depression, and attempting suicide with iodine.

Two conversations show the sharpness of Oliansky's script. Parker and Dizzy Gillespie discuss addiction: Gillespie explains to Parker how they are different – Gillespie wants to do what white people *don't expect*, he wants to represent. Parker, he says, is a "martyr." "They're gonna talk about you when you're gone, Charlie."

Similarly, when Parker is forced to go to Paris to get gigs, a musician named Benny Tate (Jason Bernard) is trying to get Parker to stay in Paris. He tells him he could be big in Paris but Parker insists he could be big at home – like Duke or Dizzy. Tate just laughs; and Parker says – so what you're sayin' is "Duke and Dizzy on one side; junkies on the other."

Most film music bios seem rushed as they plow through overly familiar greatest hits and woodenly recite the well-known ups and downs of a performer's life. *Bird* gives you a grand sense of just what Parker forged in music, and the shift from his early trials to full-blooded classic performances is rightfully startling. Not only are the musical scenes impressive, including Whitaker's take on Parker's physical presence, but the film even has the sense to slow way, way down for a scene where a strung-out Parker and a bedraggled Red Rodney are sitting around as Parker relays the exact date, time and place where he discovered his style while backing up a jazz singer.

Another well done and portentous moment: Chan is driving Charlie to a gig when a song comes on the radio: it's a Charlie Parker sax solo turned into a jazz / pop lyric. Chan is sarcastic and cynical, letting Parker know it is inferior to his solo; but Parker seems enthralled – the lyrics are speaking about him, about his death, how they "will take me back to Kansas City when I die." "Chan," Parker says when the song is over, "when I die, please don't let them take me to Kansas City."

Bird was so unlike anything Eastwood had done up to this point that it suggests a non-auteurist assumption. This is how good a movie can be when a great script is put in the hands of some starved technicians under the direction of a hack director. It's hard to say exactly what Eastwood supplied to this film as a personality other than allowing his production company to produce something different. In other words, the movie's success falls largely in the hand of scriptwriter Joel Oliansky. Up until *Bird*, there had seldom been any need to single out a script writer – given the results. Looking at the films made by Clint Eastwood before *Bird*, great scenes are almost non-existent, let alone any great sequences. If *Bird* was actually any indication of Eastwood growing into a major artist's role, wouldn't it have been evident in his next decade of movies?

Unforgiven – 1992

Late in Clint Eastwood's career as a director, critics would tentatively suggest thematic threads and recurring motifs in his movies. Many of these critics show a strange reluctance to discuss the sordid preoccupations that often pump up the films. Anti-authoritarian predilections and a reoccurrence of wayward children will be cited as examples of a mind at work. Up until 1992, it was hard to take serious cinematic or auteurist interest in Eastwood's career – *Bird* being a notable exception. *Unforgiven* clarifies the problem. Eastwood is at his best when somebody else is doing the thinking. In this case, that would be screenwriter David Peoples.

In his younger days, William Munny (Eastwood) was a drunken, vicious, murdering outlaw responsible for the deaths of men, women and children. He reached repentance of sorts when he met his wife who helped him stop drinking and made him see the errors of his ways. We meet Munny after his wife has passed away and he is left to raise two children on a small, isolated hog farm in Kansas. Munny's enterprise is on the verge of collapse; his hogs have come down with fever, and he is desperate for money.

The son of one of Munny's former desperado partners shows up at the farm. He calls himself the Schofield Kid (Jaimz Woolvett) and brags about his killing exploits. He's heading to Wyoming. A bounty of a thousand dollars has been offered for the murder of two cattle drivers responsible for a brutal attack on a woman – he tells Munny the woman's face was cut up, her ears cut off, her eyes gouged out. He's hoping Munny will partner up for half the cash.

Munny declines the offer, tells the Kid he's not like that anymore. The Kid leaves without him.

The town in Wyoming the Kid is heading for is Big Whiskey. Law and order in Big Whiskey is provided by Sheriff "Little Bill" Daggett (Gene Hackman) and a group of capable deputies played by Jeremy Rachford, John Ferguson, Ron White, Jefferson Mappin.

Big Whiskey's whorehouse is run by Skinny Dubois (Anthony James). His workers include the headstrong overseer Strawberry Alice (Frances Fisher), Little Sue (Tara Frederik), Delilah (Anna Levine), Silky (Beverly Elliott), and Faith (Lisa Repo-Martell). It is these women who offer the thousand-dollar bounty, but the story is slightly different than the one the Schofield Kid told Munny. Delilah had an altercation with a customer named Quick Mike (David Mucci). When she joked about his manhood, he became unhinged, beat her and cut up her face with a knife (her ears and eyes are intact). Sheriff Little Bill arrived and corralled Quick Mike and his partner Davey Bunting (Rob Campbell). The women wanted them both hanged though Davey had nothing to do with it. Little Bill threatened to horse whip them, but changed his mind when he found out they were cattle drivers. He let them go free but is expecting them to return in the spring with horses for Skinny Dubois to make things right. Outraged at the lack of justice the women began looking for hired killers.

Back at the farm things are falling apart. William Munny decides his only option is to pursue the bounty. He leaves his kids behind and stops in to see an old outlaw friend named Ned Logan (Morgan Freeman). Ned decides to ride along with Munny. They soon catch up to the Schofield Kid.

Back in Big Whiskey, Skinny finds out about the bounty and warns Sheriff Little Bill. They worry about bounty hunters coming into town. The first to show up is the notorious gunfighter English Bob (a witty performance by Richard Harris). Along with him is a pulp novel writer named W.W. Beauchamp (Saul Rubinek). Beauchamp is chronicling English Bob's exploits in a series of books. Unfortunately, one of Little Bill's pet peeves is people carrying guns into Big Whiskey. He and his deputies force English Bob to disarm. Little Bill then beats English Bob mercilessly and sends him packing.

Soon after, Munny, Ned and the Kid show up at Skinny's place. Little Bill gets wind that the strangers are in town and have shown up at Skinny's. Little Bill finds Munny downstairs at a table in the bar, shivering with fever. Munny has become ill after traveling in a rain storm. Ned and the Kid are upstairs dallying with the girls. Little Bill manages to get Munny's gun then gives him the same kind of beating he gave English Bob. Munny barely manages to crawl out of the saloon in one piece. Ned and the Kid escape out of the upstairs window. They join Munny, who has found his horse, and ride out of town.

They hole up outside city limits. Munny seems on the verge of dying. The cut-up whore Delilah tends to him. Ned and the Kid give up on Munny and decide to seek the cattle drivers by themselves. Munny finally gets better thanks to the attention from Delilah and the women. He joins Ned and the Kid and they track the cattle drivers to a gully where they are struggling with some steers. From the hill above, Ned pulls his rifle, and shoots Davey's horse which falls on Davey and breaks his leg. Ned takes aim on Davey but loses his nerve and can't fire. The Schofield Kid has proven himself practically blind, so Munny is left with the task of killing Davey. Davey manages to pull himself from under his horse, and crawls slowly for shelter. Munny begins firing. He finally hits Davey just before he makes it to a big boulder. Munny, Ned and the Kid retreat.

Ned decides he wants nothing more of it. He takes leave, and heads back to Kansas.

Munny and the Kid track down Quick Mike hiding at a ranch. They wait patiently for Mike by the outhouse. He finally shows up. The Kid kicks in the outhouse door and shoots him point blank. Deed done, they are ready to collect the bounty.

As they wait in a barren field under a tree for one of the women to bring the reward, the Kid expresses remorse and decides killing isn't for him. When one of the prostitutes arrives with the money, she tells them that a posse caught Ned. He was taken back to Little Bill and beaten, tortured and forced to confess. Everybody now knows the stranger is the notorious William Munny who killed women and children in a train robbery. She tells them that Ned's body is on display outside of Skinny's establishment. This infuriates Munny. She leaves. Munny begins drinking whiskey for the first time in years. He instructs the Kid to go back to Kansas, check on his children, give some of the money to Ned's wife.

Then he heads to Big Whiskey for the final confrontation with Little Bill and his men.

The screenwriter is David Webb Peoples and it is a rich, interlocked, imaginative rumination on American movie heroes and villains. Peoples has had an interesting film career. Co-writer of the acclaimed documentary *The Day Before Trinity* and author of the films *Blade Runner*, *Twelve Monkeys*, *Hero*, and *Leviathan*, as well as the *Twelve Monkeys* television series, his work at its best carries an impressive literary density and imaginative attention to character detail. There are themes present in *Unforgiven* strictly related to the excellence of Peoples' story-telling. For instance:

- At the beginning of the film, Munny is haunted by a murder he committed. He reminds Ned of a rounder he shot. "His teeth went through the back of his head. He didn't deserve that for what he did." Later on, when Little Bill is wounded and lying on the floor, Munny aims his rifle at Little Bill's head. "I don't deserve this," Little Bill says. "I'm building a house." Munny's answer: "Deserve has nothing to do with it."

- The theme of moral shiftiness is presented consistently through the film – not Western movie morality, but morality itself. In some ways, Little Bill *didn't* deserve to die, no more than the innocent rounder. And this is all connected to Bill's strange comment about his house:

- Little Bill is building a house but it's not a very good house. As one of his deputies says "You know, he don't have a straight angle on that whole god-damned porch, or the whole house for that matter. He is the worst damn carpenter." Later on, the pulp novel writer Beauchamp is at Bill's house. It is raining outside and the roof is leaking. Pots and pans are set up all over the place to catch the rain. Beauchamp remarks, "You ought to hang the carpenter." Little Bill is angered by the remark and turns to Beauchamp: "What did you say?" "I said you ought to hang the carpenter." "I am the carpenter," Little Bill yells at him.

- The idea of law, the attempts to harness it for the general good, and attendant moral leakage is given a vivid visual metaphor in Bill's preoccupation with his house. He hopes someday to work out the bugs and retire to the front porch. As corrupt as he is, he seems sincere in bringing law and order to Big Whiskey – he absolutely draws the line at bringing guns into town, for instance. Unfortunately, he's as incompetent a lawmaker as he is carpenter.

- Which brings us back to what people deserve. The first cattle driver killed by Munny is one of the few sympathetic characters in the film. He had nothing to do with the attack on Delilah and tried to make amends by bringing Delilah her own personal pony. None of this makes a difference. Davey is murdered violently and needlessly by Munny at the encouragement of the women, who should have discerned the difference between Quick Mike and Davey, even if Munny, Ned and the Kid never bothered to look into the details. When Munny finds out that the attacked woman is a whore, and her eyes and ears were not damaged, it doesn't change his mission. He isn't interested in parsing the problem – he wants the money. The women themselves are relentless in their pursuit of frontier justice. Oddly, only the disfigured Delilah shows reservations about the murders.

- Little Bill and his deputies are trying to enforce some form of order on the town, but they don't appear to be doing it by any rule of law other than what's in Little Bill's mind. When the deputies and Skinny Dubois are killed by Munny, they may not have been perfect but it's hard to say they got what they "deserved."

- Peoples makes good use of Beauchamp. Saul Rubinek gives a wormy performance of a man captivated by violence, enraptured by a vision of blood and gore. He's an exploiter – he could stand in for the director of this movie – looking for any shred of over-the-top sensationalism that might captivate the rubes and make him some money. When Little Bill deflates English Bob's reputation and obliterates him in the street, Beauchamp immediately shifts to being Little Bill's biographer. Little Bill provides a richer vein of mythical bs.

We see a marked change in Little Bill once Beauchamp starts taking notes for posterity. Little Bill begins parading around, speaking portentously, looking askance at Beauchamp, making sure he's jotting it all down. The screenwriter is deft at suggesting that at some point this is no longer a faithfully detailed Western yarn, but one that is being inflated by the governance of the man who is writing about it. At the end of the movie when the usually quiet Munny has killed everybody, does he really ride out into the street and proclaim "You better bury Ned right!... Better not cut up, nor otherwise harm no whores... or I'll come back and kill every one of you sons of bitches." Or is this just a big ending imagined by Beauchamp himself.

During the scenes of violence when Little Bill is kicking the crap out of somebody, beating them to a bloody pulp, the bystanders – which include the prostitutes and the deputies – are barely able to look at the carnage. It's a suitable comparison to an Eastwood audience, though at least in the case of Strawberry Alice and her girls – they are getting what they paid for.

Peoples probably also deserves credit for the brief yet effective characterizations given the deputies and the prostitutes. This is great ensemble work and credit has to be given to the cameraman (Jack N. Green) for the intimate set-ups, the editor (Joel Cox) quickly capturing all the ephemeral moments, and Eastwood himself for orchestrating it all. Henry Bumstead's sets are as captivating as ever but unhampered by the tendency of Eastwood to overuse them to the point of making them look stodgily theatrical. Here the sets are intertwined with movement through pastoral settings. The scene where Munny and the Schofield Kid are waiting to collect their bounty under a tree in the middle of nowhere and, in the distance, they see a rider coming, then continue their conversation as the rider moves slowly closer – it's the kind of patience with time, space and mood that Eastwood is seldom interested in.

Million Dollar Baby - 2004

Million Dollar Baby hasn't the originality of films from the same year like *Eternal Sunshine of the Spotless Mind, Before Sunset, Collateral, I Heart Huckabees, Life Aquatic with Steve Zissou* or *Spider Man 2*, but it certainly gets most of the job done. Well-directed and well-written, at least until the change of pace in the last third, the movie landed four *Academy Awards*: Best Picture, Best Director (Eastwood), Best Actress in a Leading Role (Hilary Swank), Best Actor in a Supporting Role (Morgan Freeman).

Frankie Dunn (Eastwood) is a seasoned boxing manager who owns a run-down gym in Los Angeles. He's maneuvering a successful boxer named Big Willie Little (Mike Colter) towards a championship fight. Ex-prize-fighter Eddie Dupris (Morgan Freeman), an old friend of Frankie's, works around the gym as a live-in trainer, maintenance man and trouble-shooter.

Frankie is devastated when Big Willie Little leaves him for another manager. Disgruntled and depressed, Frankie isn't too interested when Maggie Fitzgerald (Hilary Swank) begins practicing at the gym and begs him to manage her. Frankie shuns Maggie, but Eddie gives her some fighting tips. Maggie's focus impresses Eddie and he gently tries to persuade Frankie to take a look at her progress. Eventually, Frankie caves in to her persistent pleadings. He lets her know that he'll train her, but once she's ready, she'll have to get somebody else for a manager.

When Maggie is ready for her first fight, Frankie turns her over to a different manager. Frankie and Eddie attend the boxing match, and Eddie lets Frankie know he thinks it's a set-up - that the manager wants Maggie to lose so he can gain favor with another manager. When Maggie begins to lose badly, Frankie takes over as ringside coach and gives her some advice. When she wins, he decides to manager her.

By 2004, Eastwood's face had taken on the look of a gargoyle, complete with faded, sealed-over eyes and flinty architecture. He fits the role nicely. More importantly, Swank girds Maggie with a well-spring of self-destructive working-class desperation - she recognizes the closest thing to a talent she has is hitting a punching bag and she clings to it for dear life.

Maggie ends up being a natural, and the boxing scenes are among the best I've seen. They are without the hide-the-actual fight problems of many boxing films. When these girls hit the canvas, it looks like they hit it hard. Even better, Maggie's rise towards the championship is done in a way that you feel the ascendancy. First, she gains a reputation for knocking out minor fighters in the first round, then Frankie has to pay managers because nobody wants to fight her. When Maggie advances in class, you see the fights getting a little harder - she gets her nose broken in her first major fight. Soon she's traveling the world. When she gets back home, she finally lands a championship fight against a boxer known to fight dirty. Maggie barely manages to prevail in the fight, but as she turns to go to her corner after the bell has sounded, the fighter hits her from behind; she's knocked down and breaks her neck on the corner stool.

In the aftermath, Maggie is quadriplegic. Hospitalized, her hillbilly relatives attempt to coerce her to sign over her savings. Frankie is her guardian angel, he attempts to find better doctors, suggests ways she can go to school. After doctors amputate Maggie's leg, she decides she wants to die.

She feels like she's accomplished what she wanted in life and asks Frankie to kill her. He refuses, but Maggie attempts to do herself in by biting her tongue viciously, and her problems under constant sedation make him change his mind.

It's probably a good indication of how Hilary Swank's performance affected people that some critics expressed problems with the grim ending of the film. A writer at *The Weekly Standard* actually said Eastwood should have let her become an "inspirational spokesman." Eastwood's suggestion that the film was about "the American Dream" has some merit, but the last third of the film is an American nightmare. The film is about boxing aspirations, a young woman's struggle to break out of small-town poverty; but in the third act the movie suddenly shifts to a film about mercy killing. It's a jarring transition.

Andrew Sarris found the film "depressing." He was frustrated that "critics have scrupulously avoided going into detail on the sudden pile-up of misfortunes that supposedly makes Mr. Eastwood's film so moving." The third act is encapsulated to death. Settling into such a stark change-up demands some kind of continuance of the story, but it stops in its tracks. Sarris wondered, "how a championship fight that ended in a quasi-criminal act fails to illicit any repercussions or protests, by Frankie or anyone else." Maggie disappears, a bed-ridden cipher, while Eastwood continues looking for an *Academy Award* amongst all the gruesome reality. Maggie's argument that she has been a success and would prefer that she died on top of the game could at least have been supported by a hint of her worth in the sporting world - by fans, by letters, and with some sense that her accomplishment carried some importance. Eastwood loses the thread when he loses the bigger picture and the film becomes closet melodrama. The dirty details of the police investigation that would have obviously followed Maggie's demise is not even suggested. At some point you just have to end the damn film.

Flags of Our Fathers - 2006

The bracketing is similar to Spielberg's *Saving Private Ryan*: Plaintive reminiscences begin and end the film; a protracted military assault is the crux of the action. Paul Haggis and William Boyles, Jr. are credited with the script. Part of the film is a taut, no-nonsense depiction of World War II battle. The rest of the film deals with the controversy surrounding the planting of the U.S. flag atop Mt. Suribachi on the Japanese held island of Iwo Jima and the iconic photograph that was thought to have captured the event. The initial tight focus on a single military unit as it advances on a small island gives the audience a clear sense of a powerful force moving inland. The visual effects supervised by Michael Owens and the editing by Joel Cox are skillful in the way they depict 101 ways to meet a horrible death while attacking a Japanese island.

The film starts with an elderly WW II veteran, Doc Bradley (George Grizzard), suffering a heart attack and his son subsequently delving into his past experience in Iwo Jima. This leads to some voice-overs explaining how "soldiers didn't like to talk about their experiences," or "soldiers didn't fight to be heroes: they fought to protect the people in front of them and the people behind them." The narration attempts to force your thoughts into a direction of faux-masculinity and hymn-backed self-sacrifice that doesn't blend well with a film that, after all, is about a military deception laced with phony politicians and bullying Army propagandists.

We meet the soldiers on board a battleship heading to Iwo Jima. You get familiar with the soldiers before they put on their battle helmets and start blending in with the scenery - which is shot in washed-out tones tinged with blue hues. The unit is presented as a bunch of wholesome American youngsters - there is none of the harsh delineations of past war films - depressive suicidal loners like Steven McQueen in *Hell is For Heroes*, fractious issues of race and sadism in films like *The Steel Helmet*; issues of class or brainwashing as in *Paths of Glory* or *Full Metal Jacket*; the metaphorical personality conflicts of *Platoon*; or the spiritual proclivities of *The Thin Red Line*. The film focuses to a large extent on the group involved in the flag-raising controversy: the Native American Ira Hayes (Adam Beach), Rene Gagnon (Jesse Bradford), Medic "Doc" Bradley (Ryan Phillippe), Sergeant Michael Strank (Barry Pepper), Corporal Harlon Block (Benjamin Walker), and Private First-Class Franklin Sousley (Joseph Cross).

As the unit advances quickly and dutifully up Mt. Suribachi we are given the point of view of the hidden Japanese soldiers in their bunkers swinging big guns towards the unsuspecting troops. This first wave of slaughter is a compelling display of cannon fodder. A paranoid nervousness is evoked. At one point a Japanese soldier throws himself into Ira Hayes' foxhole only to find himself hoisted on a bayoneted rifle like a flag above Ira's head. Elsewhere a soldier in a seemingly secure foxhole is whisked away underground and tortured. At another point, we see a head go bouncing across a soldier's body. There's a quintessential cinematic moment when a radioman is calling in targets and the radio gets shot away from his ear and he starts yelling "Give me a radio; give me a radio" which is quickly replaced and pulled to his ear only to be cruelly dispatched along with radioman himself. Barry Pepper's Sgt. Strank has the strongest physical presence in the film - a lead-by-example performance that carries a poetically fearless edge in a picturesque death scene. The battle scenes are the best action scenes Eastwood has filmed.

In the aftermath of the battle, the photograph of the flag being raised atop Mt. Suribachi goes viral in American newspapers. The American public is unaware the circulated photo is a re-shoot of the actual flag-raising and that different people were used for the new photo. Ira Hayes, Doc Bradley and Rene Gagnon are picked to do an American tour for U.S. War Bonds with the flag iconography as the backdrop. The men are exploited by politicians and businessmen along the way. The businessmen are despicable - using what sound like old Eastwood phrases (i.e., one businessman to Ira: "did you kill them with a tomahawk, Chief?"). Ira Hayes in particular is emotionally affected by the fraud, and stricken by the fact that his friend Harlon Block (Benjamin Walker) who was killed in battle is not rightfully designated as one of the flag raisers.

The film is not quite an epic. Eastwood rushes scenes in later years depicting the death of a drunken Ira Hayes, the PTSD of Doc Bradley, and the inability of Gagnon to land anything other than a janitorial job despite the promises of the rich businessmen he met on the War Bonds tour.

Though Eastwood's film attempted to set the record straight, it wasn't until after the film was released that another soldier, PFC Harold Schultz, was recognized as taking part in the original flag hoisting. Schultz doesn't even figure in the film.

Clint Eastwood

as Auteur

Clint Eastwood as Auteur

Miscellany

1971: Play Misty for Me. 1973: *High Plains Drifter*; Breezy. 1975: Eiger Sanction. 1976: Outlaw Josey Wales. 1977: The Gauntlet. 1980: Bronco Billy. 1982: Firefox; Honkytonk Man. 1983: Sudden Impact. 1985: Pale Rider. 1986: Heartbreak Ridge. 1988: *Bird*. 1990: White Hunter, Black Heart; The Rookie. 1992: *Unforgiven*. 1993: A Perfect World. 1995: Bridges of Madison County. 1997: Absolute Power; *Midnight in the Garden of Good and Evil*. 1999: True Crime. 2000: Space Cowboys. 2002: Blood Work. 2003: Mystic River. 2004: *Million Dollar Baby*. 2006: *Flag of Our Fathers*; Letters from Iwo Jima. 2008: Changeling; Gran Torino. 2009: Invictus. 2010: Hereafter. 2011: J. Edgar. 2014: Jersey Boys; American Sniper. 2016: Sully. 2018: The 15:17 to Paris; The Mule. 2019: Jewell. 2021: Cry Macho.

Clint Eastwood's few good movies, with the exception of *High Plains Drifter*, are successful to the extent that they ditch Eastwood's most personal inclinations. *High Plains Drifter* is the most succinct and compelling rendition of Eastwood's rampant misanthropy because the script offers no room for the meaningless digressions and audience-pandering mannerisms found in most of his films. Personal expression

169

diminished his films rather than enhanced them. It would be twenty years on and many action films later before David Peoples near-perfect script for *Unforgiven* enabled Eastwood, for the first and last time, to render guns and violence with any reflective moral seriousness.

Bird was an anomaly - a sublimely acted drama about jazz giant Charlie Parker that offered stark realism instead of the usual superman heroes, fake bureaucratic villains, serial killers, car crashes, suspiciously frequent bank robberies and idiotic fist fights.

Million Dollar Baby was one of the few times Eastwood has given major screen time to an actress and Hilary Swank gave a memorable performance as an underdog boxer whose turn in the spotlight ends in tragedy.

Bronco Billy and *Midnight in the Garden of Good and Evil* win a few points for being enjoyable but lose all points on an auteurist level because they aren't really Eastwood - they portray a world that might be a fairly nice place to live in.

J. Edgar has a dramatically interesting homosexual subplot provided by screenwriter Dustin Lance Black, but it should be pointed out that Eastwood has never been particularly good with epic scope and the movie suffers from encapsulation. That said, *Flags of Our Fathers* was a commendable war film that is probably the closest Eastwood came to a successful prestige project though it arrived exactly at the moment his films embraced tinkling self-composed movie scores and increasingly ugly color schemes.

Early on, Eastwood's primary failure was in the way he simplified the hard-boiled action film, laying on the Eastwood formula, shoving out the realism. As a result, his action stories are less varied, less sober, less well-acted than those of old school directors like Robert Aldrich, Anthony Mann, Sam Fuller, Raoul Walsh, Don Siegel and Nicholas Ray.

The difference in quality between the Siegel / Leone / Eastwood films and the Eastwood / Eastwood films suggest Eastwood wasn't the best director for his own vehicles. The successful initiation of the Eastwood archetype by Sergio Leone and Donald Siegel sent Eastwood down a rabbit hole of sensationalized action-flick contrivance, anti-liberal superficialities, and grotesque anti-social brashness. Along the way, Eastwood used "political correctness" as a boogieman to defend the sickly anti-social touches his audience expected and adored. He plied his trade a little too carelessly on the wrong side of the culture wars with little taste or intelligence to guide him. The early Eastwood templates seem increasingly dated, cheap, self-interested, marginal, artless; and his later films are simply boring.

Sources

pg. 4 - "Eastwood didn't know who ...": Mark Eliot. *American Rebel.* Harmony Books, 2009. pg. 96.

pg. 5 - "If the heroes of Ford ...": Andrew Sarris. *The American Cinema: Directors and Directions: 1929 -1968.* pg. 120.

pg. 5 – "This is the ultimate meaning ..."; Ibid. pg. 72.

pg. 5 – "Dieterle was around on ..."; Ibid. pg. 255.

pg. 6 – "one of the critics most important ...": Pauline Kael. *Film Quarterly,* Spring, 1963

pg. 7 - "A number of reviewers ...": Pauline Kael *Partisan Review,* Fall, 1962.

pg. 7 - "But what at first seems an attack ...": *Time Magazine,* June 1962.

pg. 8 – "It may be necessary to point out ...": Kael. *Film Quarterly,* Spring, 1963.

pg. 8 - "When a famous director ...": Ibid.

pg. 8 - "she was a subject of discussion ...": Eliot. *American Rebel.* pg. 168.

pg. 8 - "Kael found an avenue ...": Eastwood interview. *Video Magazine,* May, 1985.

pg. 9 - "the trucks give the performances": Kael. *For Keeps.* pg. 779.

pg. 9 - "When Eastwood puzzles over how Kael ...": Eliot. *American Rebel.* Pg. 168.

pg. 9 - "maleness...": Eliot. *American Rebel.* pg. 168.

pg. 10 - "Of all art forms ...": Pauline Kael. *I Lost it at the Movies.* pg. 217

pg. 10 – "Fighting itself is the subject...".'" Ibid. pg. 107

pg. 11 - "The Seven Samurai is the kind ...": Ibid. pg. 108-109

pg. 11 - "When violence itself becomes ...": Ibid. pg. 109-110

pg. 12 - "One rarely discussed issue ...": Seymour Hersh. *Times Literary Supplement*, June 1, 2018.

pg. 13 - "They don't even belong ... ": Pete Hammil interview with Sergio Leone. *American Film*, 1984.

pg. 26 – "war and the effect it has on people ...": Reissue of *Outlaw Josey Wales* interview on DVD - 1999.

pg. 28 - "carnage production numbers ..."; Variety June 30, 1976.

pg. 33 - "classic Clint Eastwood: fast ..."; Roger Ebert. *Chicago Sun-Times* Jan. 1, 1977

pg. 44 – "fascist medievalism ..."; Pauline Kael. *New Yorker* Jan. 15, 1972.

pg. 53 – "caresses the material as if he didn't know ...": Roger Ebert. *Chicago Sun Times*, Dec 5, 1986.

pg. 76 – "In more than a half a century ...": Peter Travers. *Rolling Stone Magazine*, Oct. 14, 2010.

pg. 77 – "I don't believe in woo-woo ...": Roger Ebert, *Chicago Sun Times*, Oct. 19, 2010.

pg. 79 - "reportedly threw up." Mark Halperin. Penguin Press, 2013. *Double Down: Game Change 2012.*

pg. 81 - "Everybody's walking on eggshells ...": *Esquire* interview; August 3, 2016.

pg. 81 - "it's a tough voice ...": Ibid.

Gonna Need a Leader Here

By Walt Wiley

Published by:
Winning With Encouragement, Inc.
Charlotte, North Carolina

Produced by:

Shelby, North Carolina

Contents

Acknowledgements

I want to thank those who have often encouraged me to write a book. Not that there have been thousands of them, but over the years that suggestion has been made to me many times.

Heading the list would be my wife Patti, who has always believed in Walt Wiley more than Walt Wiley does. After reading my rough drafts she would say, "I like this. Keep going."

Our sons Bart and Brett, who have been nothing but an encouragement to me since they have been around, have likewise encouraged me in this project. Their wives Erin and Elizabeth have always been a source of encouragement to me, and this book will be required reading for our three granddaughters … that is, as soon as they learn to read.

I would be remiss in not mentioning Dianne Agee whom I have worked with at Winning With Encouragement for many years. She not only encouraged me to put things on paper, but also laboriously typed and retyped as well as proofread the manuscript.

The Board of Directors of Winning With Encouragement: Joy, Lee, Wayne, Bill, Jim, George, Chip and Tim. They have all been a great encouragement to me in more ways than just this project.

My former colleague, David Hodge, also needs to be mentioned. The thought of a book centering on the main points of Winning With Encouragement's leadership seminar entitled **The Look of the Leader** accompanied by quotes was originally his idea. And David has always been an encouragement to me.

I also want to thank our friend Karen Wessman, proofreader extraordinaire, for her helpful insight. There were also a number of friends who read the earliest forms of this writing and offered helpful suggestions as well as encouragement.

Were these people right about encouraging me to write a book? Keep reading and then you decide. At least if you don't like the book, you now know some of the people to blame.

Preface

Repeatedly, I have been known to say that there isn't anything any of us need more than encouragement. I know, I know. You say, "That's nice, but I *need* a new job, a new car, a new house, or a new spouse," but when it's all said and done, what we really could use on a regular basis is a large dose of encouragement. To *encourage* means *to give heart to, to spur on, to motivate or incite*. Too often, the challenges of something called life call for courage and we question whether we have it in us to meet those challenges. Just at that time, someone enters our lives, helps us through those obstacles and offers us encouragement. What did they do? Simple: they gave us heart, they gave us courage. Remember, to encourage is to give heart to.

The purpose of this book is to give you courage. I want to encourage you. I want to give you heart. And I want to encourage you about a specific thing: You are more of a leader than you think you are!

I also want to remind you that there are all types of situations and people around you who could use you. It's been said that the need for leadership always exceeds the supply. That's true, but it's not because of a lack of leaders as much as it is that too few of us have mustered the courage to step into a situation and take on a leadership role. At the core of this book is the encouragement to do that.

Did you know that the Greek word for *encouragement*

can also be translated as *exhortation*?[1] Now that is an animal of a different stripe! To *exhort* means *to warn, urge, caution*. It's a much stronger word than encourage (and I personally would rather be encouraged than exhorted), but it's the same word and they both paint the same scene: someone steps into the lives of others and tells them what they need to hear.

As a teenager, I remember receiving a great job offer that I liked, but I questioned whether I could pull it off. I still remember where I was when a man I respected encouraged me to go for it and assured me that I had what it took to do it. That job ended up meaning a lot to me and I will always be grateful for his encouragement. I can also recall where I was sitting when a woman I greatly respected said these words to me, rather sternly, "When are you going to grow up and start believing in yourself?" Both scenes, both comments motivated me, spurred me on, and gave me heart, but they were done in two different ways.

I have a confession to make. Even though I am into encouragement and am associated with an organization called Winning With Encouragement, you might discover as you read that I will step into your life with more exhortation than what you would call encouragement, but all the while hoping for the same result. You see, it bothers me that there are countless people and situations all around us crying out with a sense of urgency these words, "Gonna need a leader here." If it's not a voice, it's a language that's expressed in the way they carry themselves or a facial expression that seems to be saying it can be done or we could do it if only we had someone to lead us. Look around. Open your eyes. That cry may be coming from someone at the office, in your neighborhood, at the club, in your class, those in your service organization, at your church, or perhaps coming from members of your own household … "Gonna need a leader here!"

In Chapter 8 in the Book of Acts (in the New Testament of the Bible), a man named Philip crosses paths with an Egyptian government official who is sitting in his chariot reading the Bible. Philip asked him, "Do you understand what you are reading?" The Egyptian spoke for every person who has a desire to understand or who can visualize what he could be. He is a clear representative of one who can see what needs to be done, who wants to accomplish something, who wants to do something significant, who wants to be a part of something that works, who wants to make it happen or wants to see improvements. He simply said, "How can I understand unless someone guides me?" [2]

In this book I am going to encourage—no, I am going to *exhort* you—to look around and give careful attention to people and situations desperately in need of a leader. They are not difficult to find. They are all around, and they need someone to provide for them what they won't or perhaps are unable to supply for themselves.

The outline of the contents of this book will follow material from a Winning With Encouragement teaching called *The Look of the Leader*. The study features leadership concepts from the life of a man named Nehemiah, whose story is found, of all places, in the Old Testament of the Bible. Over the past decade principles of leadership from this seminar have been taught to thousands worldwide.

Each section of the book contains small portions of the major points and flow of *The Look of the Leader*, but by no means is it my attempt to teach the full content of the seminar. To be exposed to the complete teaching, contact us at Winning With Encouragement.

The Quotes

In my quest to motivate you, spur you on and incite you to action, I have included over 200 inspirational, motivational and thought-provoking quotes. You will love them and will be able to use them with other people. Some of them are the same ones used throughout *The Look of the Leader*. Some are from individuals you've never heard of. Some are from people whose names you will recognize, and many of them are ones that complement the ideas and principles espoused in the seminar.

So enjoy. Do I hope you are encouraged and/or exhorted?

Yes!

Walt Wiley

Introduction On
LEADERSHIP
You are more of a leader than you think you are!

Too few people see themselves as leaders. But get this: Regardless of your age or your station in life, there is a more than excellent possibility that you are either in a *leadership position* or in a *position of leadership*.

A *leadership position* denotes an assignment that has been formally presented to you. It comes with a job description and in all probability a title and certain demands or expectations. It is often something sought and even celebrated when it has been offered. Likewise, there is an excellent chance that as a result of that position your office grew larger. There's the possibility that you had an increase in compensation and perks. Maybe your parking spot was moved closer to the building. Maybe you even received a key to the executive lunch room. These are just a few things that would possibly indicate that a person has attained a leadership position.

It should be noted that being in a leadership position does not necessarily make you an effective leader. Unfortunately, there are numerous people in leadership positions who are not necessarily first-rate leaders.

Now be careful not to confuse a leadership position with what I am calling a *position of leadership*. Positions of leadership denote countless unclaimed or vacant opportunities all around us. They represent groups of people who are like sheep without a shepherd, hoping—even begging—for someone to come along and step in and help make happen what they all talk about and what they dream of. Those positions have no bounds in age, education, experience or personality. Your family is looking for a leader, or maybe it's the people you hang out with at the office or at school – anyone who needs a voice, direction or someone to take charge. It's a position of leadership where a group of people are ready to go but they only lack one thing: a leader.

Think about it: opportunities I am calling positions of leadership can come to you in various ways. For instance, an 80-year-old man named Moses was minding his own business tending sheep in the Midian desert when he noticed a bush that was burning and yet not being consumed. When he went to check it out, the bush spoke to him. It was God calling him to leave where he was and return to Egypt to lead God's children away from their oppression. Moses was clearly called by God to step into a position of leadership he never dreamed of and was reluctant to pursue. After some soul searching, he eventually responded to what he realized was a call on his life. By doing this he encountered numerous challenges, but he also experienced a fulfilling satisfaction that only comes with being right where you are suppose to be.

Yes, some people are called into positions of leadership.

David, on the other hand, was just a kid taking lunch to his brothers who were serving in the Israeli army doing battle with their arch rival, the Philistines. When he arrived in the Valley of Elah, he became conscious of an position of leadership. Some are called, while others simply have their antennas up and their eyes open, and as a result come face to face with something that has to be done. David jumped into a dangerous situation, felled the 9-foot giant named Goliath, and that simply propelled him on to bigger and better things. Don't allow your lack of awareness to rob you of being conscious of a place that needs you. Some are called, and some are simply conscious of someone or something calling out for a leader.

Thirdly and perhaps the most obvious position of leadership is one that you created. You made a decision to marry, perhaps have brought children into the world, maybe started a company, or even volunteered to coach the Little League baseball team. Guess what? Those things were your idea and each one of them is an obvious position of leadership, none of which you can turn your back on.

There are two problems that exist with positions of leadership. One is that too often these positions remain vacant; that is, no one takes the responsibility to organize, plan, direct, motivate or inspire others. Secondly, even if someone has assumed the role of leader in those environments, neither they nor the others with them necessarily recognize it as leadership when, in fact, it is.

For instance, the subdivision where you live organizes a cleanup day where all the inhabitants are asked to pledge 2-3 hours on a certain Saturday morning to spruce up the public entrance, gather the debris that has accumulated on the grounds over the past months, and even paint the fence.

Much to everyone's surprise and delight, 15-18 homes are represented that Saturday morning and everyone present appears ready to pitch in and help. Can you picture the scene as everyone gathers? Typically, the first 30 minutes has everyone standing around, staring at the ground, mumbling softly to anyone they know, nodding hello to others, while nothing happens. Finally, Rachel speaks up and organizes the group into spunky, let's-get-this-place-cleaned-up groups. Rachel took advantage of a position of leadership.

Many unfortunately would not see what Rachel did as leadership. Why is that? It's because of the prevailing misconceptions surrounding the title of leader. Let me list a few of what I would call leadership misconceptions:

1. Personality

Leadership takes a certain personality. We think a good leader must be aggressive, demanding, controlling, authoritative, and bordering on being dictatorial. Rachel was a nice, sweet lady who got things done, but she possessed none of those attributes. Too often, we assume the people who do the most talking and who confidently and boldly express their ideas make the best leaders. Having those qualities certainly does not disqualify a person from being an obvious leader, but in order to effectively lead others, do you have to be like that? Do the superior leaders all have to possess a George Patton-like bravado? I think not.

2. Size

I am not referring to the size of the person, although I am convinced many people have a picture in their mind of how the perfect leader should look. It's amazing the criteria we use with regard to size, looks, charisma, dress, or something such as posture. But that's another story. No, I am referring to the size of the project. Somehow we have concluded that the larger the enterprise, the better the leadership. We would identify good leaders based on the number of people who report to them or the size of the organization, school or company they command. How could you conclude that Rachel may have been an effective leader when there were only 19 people there to work with her? Don't conclude that a person isn't a leader because his company is small or there are only 7 people in her department. That's not fair and neither is it true. Individuals seriously working at leadership roles in their small families may not receive applause or get much recognition, but it will be replaced with satisfaction and gratification that will last a lifetime. Are good leaders only the ones who direct large numbers of people? Again, I think not.

3. Recognition

Have you noticed that people identify good leaders based on what they have heard, read, or possibly seen on television? "She must be a good leader. Oprah said so when she featured her on her show." Or, "He must be a good leader. Everyone has heard of him and he has been around for a long time." Or maybe, "Certainly he's a great leader. I saw a write-up on him in a popular magazine and on Facebook." Or even, "A good leader? Are you kidding? His name is on the side of the building and everyone knows him."

In the book, *Good to Great*, author Jim Collins identifies 11 of the top companies in our country today and analyzes the traits that have given them staying power. Amazingly, after stating the value of good leadership, the author confesses that a unique characteristic of each of these known and successful companies is the fact that few people know who the leaders are.

Be careful that you don't base your definition of effective leadership on recognizing who is in charge. Collins said, "These leaders are comfortable with the idea that most people don't even know that the roots of that success trace back to their efforts." Then the author quotes one of these leaders saying, "I want to look out from my porch at one of the great companies of the world someday and be able to say, 'I used to work there'." [1]

At the front entrance of the subdivision that Saturday

morning, very few people knew Rachel. But when she took charge and gave direction, things started to happen and under her leadership the job was done in 2½ hours. Without this unknown lady the group might still be standing there mumbling to each other.

4. Wealth

Have you noticed that we are prone to assume rich people are good leaders, or have you observed the tendency to place people who have a lot of money in leadership positions? They must be good leaders; look at their worth. Is Donald Trump a good leader? Of course, he is. Look at all he has built and what he possesses. And besides, he is a take-charge guy, not afraid to fire people. Mr. Trump may be a good leader, but are those the qualifications for such a title?

5. Leaders versus managers

We are prone to identify a person as a good leader when, in reality, he or she is an excellent manager. The difference between leaders and managers is too vast for this publication, but, suffice it to say, leaders provide vision while managers supply perspectives. Leaders are always on the lookout for opportunities; managers strive for accomplishments. Good managers are extremely important to any endeavor, but that does not necessarily mean they are good leaders.

It is my conjecture that there are countless people in positions of leadership who are doing an outstanding job. They may not be leading large organizations, there may not be great fanfare accompanying their accomplishments, but they have successfully handled a position of leadership or a leadership position.

I also believe that more people need to stop thinking about who and what qualifies one to be a leader and take advantage of that position of leadership presently staring them in the face. They need to jump in and become the voice that the family, the department, the store, the neighborhood, or the project so desperately lacks. They need to realize they do not have to take on a new personality, become something they are not, or lead something of notoriety. We need people to refrain from sitting on the sidelines and instead look for and grasp hold of that position of leadership that is there for the taking.

Have you noticed that leadership as it is defined today focuses on the person in charge and the project he or she is leading? We make our judgments on who and what: who is doing it and what they are doing. We find ourselves enamored with people based on those two things. You might hear, "Sure, she's an excellent leader. Don't you know who she is? After all, she's the founder, the president and the chairperson." Or you might hear this, "Of course, he's a great leader. Look at the size of the company or the number of people who report to him." We frequently judge leadership with no regard to how they go about it or how they have treated their people.

This attitude also has the propensity to influence the leaders as well. Their self-worth is often tied to who they are and what they do. They get caught up in all the notoriety and continue to surround themselves with 'yes' followers, causing them to lose sight of reality. The 'don't-make-waves' followers supply very little accountability and they excuse courses of action. What they believe to be questionable practices are never confronted because of who was responsible for it and how it benefited the company's bottom line.

I declare to you: Leadership is not based on who you are and what you do; it is based on *how*—how you do it, how you conduct business, how you treat the people you lead, and how you direct your own personal life.

Now don't get me wrong. This is not to infer that who you are and what you do is inconsequential. After all, you have been specially created by God, and after He was done He admired what He had produced ... you! You are special. What you do also matters. You have been created in God's image and have been gifted by Him. He has plans for you. Hopefully, you have considered all of that and know for certain you are doing exactly what He created you to do. Yes, who and what are important; however, I repeat, it is how you go about doing things that give us a strong glimpse into the real you.

The real measure of men or women is not always

obvious when all you are able to see is who they are and what they do. If you want a glimpse of a person's heart—the real person—it can best be measured by how he or she does things. If I told you who I am and what I do, what do you really know about me? Very, very little. But if you watch how I go about life, how I conduct myself, how I treat others, how I act and react, it will reveal volumes about me.

This book will outline leadership traits that reveal what it takes to organize a group of people and get something accomplished, but not without paying close attention to how the person goes about it.

Attempting to find leaders today who are more concerned about doing things the right way as opposed to enhancing their own image or their wallets is not that easy. Where can we go to discover a leader who is more concerned about how as opposed to who and what?

Interestingly, there is an excellent story of extraordinary leadership found in the life of a man named Nehemiah in the book of the Bible that bears his name. He was not in a leadership position. How could he be? He worked for an insecure, dictatorial man who just happened to be the leader of the mightiest nation of his time, Persia. However, when Nehemiah became aware of something that needed fixing, he did not shy away from what was an obvious and unique position of leadership.

Join me in examining his life and his story as he takes

advantage of a position of leadership he was not looking for and leads a group of strangers on an adventurous path of excitement and accomplishment they will never forget. Who is he? Nehemiah. What did he do? He led a group of strangers to construct a wall that had been broken down for over 70 years, and together they accomplished the task in the midst of difficult circumstances in 52 days. That's who he was and what he did, but the real leadership lesson from Nehemiah is gleaned when you carefully watch how he did it.

So you will know where I am coming from, please allow me to give you my own personal definition of leadership:

Leadership is successfully directing others in a project while having them fulfilled and God honored.

Oh, and one more thing: Look around … where are you needed? Where is that position of leadership with your name on it? You have been watching it and have been concerned about it. You know you should do something about it. Where is that group of people gathered who are seeking satisfaction, success, victory, answers, excitement and fulfillment who only lack one thing? They are the ones crying out, "Gonna need a leader here." Why can't that leader be you?

LEADERSHIP
Motivating and inspiring quotes from others

The demand for leadership always exceeds the supply.
—Unknown

The loss of the leader or the birth of misgivings about him/her brings on the outbreak of panic.
—Sigmund Freud

If you're riding ahead of the herd, take a look back every now and then to make sure it's still there.
—Will Rogers

If you want to be the leader of a large following, just obey the speed limit on a winding two-lane road.
—Charles Farr

You don't manage people, you manage things. You lead people.
—Admiral Grace Hooper

Being in power is like being a lady.
If you have to remind people you are, you aren't.
—Margaret Thatcher

I never thought in terms of being a leader.
I thought in terms of helping people.
—John Hume

The true leader is always interested in finding the
best way to accomplish something rather than having
his or her own way.
—John Wooden

Biblical leadership is more for the benefit of the followers—not the enrichment of the leader.
—Unknown

Twenty years from now you will be more disappointed by the things you didn't do than by the things you did do.
—Mark Twain

We must be silent before we can listen.
We must listen before we can learn.
We must learn before we can prepare.
We must prepare before we can serve.
We must serve before we can lead.
—William Arthur Ward

The goal of many leaders is to get people to think more highly of the leader.
The goal of a great leader is to help people to think more highly of themselves.
—J. Carta Nortcutt

True leadership means to receive power from God and to use it under God's rule to serve people in God's way.
—Leighton Ford

A great leader comes along about once in a generation and great problems come along about three times a week.
—Unknown

When God measures a man, He puts the tape around his heart, not his head.
—Unknown

As in water face reveals face, so a man's heart reveals the man.
—Proverbs 27:19

Leaders we admire do not place themselves at the center; they place others there. They do not seek the attention of people; they give it to others. They do not focus on satisfying their own aims and desires; they look for ways to respond to the needs and interests of their constituents. They are not self-centered; they concentrate on the constituent.

—James Kouzes and Barry Posner
The Leadership Challenge

I believe that the most effective leaders are people who are servants of other people, especially from a biblical point of view. Expending your energy and resources in the interest of others can be exhausting, but biblically speaking, this is how we're called to invest our lives.

—Kenneth Boa

The successful leader is the one who makes the right move at the right time with the right motive.
—Unknown

Leadership is the most studied yet least understood of all the social sciences.
—**Ken Gangel**

A leader is someone who knows where he is going and is able to persuade others to go along with him.
—**Howard Hendricks**

Leadership is the capacity
and will to rally men and women
to a common purpose
and the character
which inspires confidence.
—**Bernard Law Montgomery**

Leadership is inspiring others.
—**Charles Swindoll**

Leadership is based on a spiritual quality:
the power to inspire others to follow.
—Vince Lombardi

Leadership is the ability to get men to do what they
don't want to do and like it.
—Harry Truman

Leadership is not magnetic
personality—that can just as well
be a glib tongue. It is not making
friends and influencing people—
that is flattery. Leadership is lifting a
person's vision to higher sights, the
raising of a person's performance
to a higher standard, the building
of a personality beyond its normal
limitations.
—Peter Drucker

Leadership is the process of persuasion or example by which an individual induces a group to pursue objectives held by the leader or shared by his/her followers.
—John W. Gardner

He who thinketh he leadeth and hath no one following him is only out for a walk.
—Leadership Proverb

To be a leader you have to make people want to follow you, and nobody wants to follow someone who doesn't know where he is going.
—Joe Namath

All of the great leaders have had one characteristic in common: it was the willingness to confront unequivocally the major anxiety of their people in their time.
—John Kenneth Galbraith

Leadership is influence.
—John Maxwell

Some of the best business and nonprofit CEOs I've worked with over a 65-year consulting career were not stereotypical leaders. They were all over the map in terms of their personalities, attitudes, values, strengths, and weaknesses.
—Peter Drucker

Leadership is a stewardship; it's temporary and you're accountable.
—Andy Stanley

I must hurry for there they go and I am their leader.
—Unknown

A leader is one who influences a specific group of people to move in a God-given direction.
—**J. Robert Clinton**

The purpose of influence is to speak up for those who have no influence.
—**Rick Warren**

Control is not leadership; management is not leadership; leadership is leadership.
—**Dee Hock**

Leadership is the ability of a single individual through his or her actions to motivate others to higher levels of achievement.
—**Buck Rodgers**

Leadership and learning
are indispensable
to each other.
—John F. Kennedy

We define leadership as a skill of influencing people
to work enthusiastically toward goals identified as
being for the common good.
—James C. Hunter

The successful leader gets superior performance from
ordinary people.
—Al Kaltman

I consider leadership to be the exercise of one's
special gifts under the call of God to serve a certain
group of people in achieving the goals God has given
them toward the end of glorifying Christ.
—Ken Gangel

It is the capacity to develop and improve their skills that distinguishes leaders from followers.
—**Warren Bennis**

Everything rises and falls on leadership.
—**John Maxwell**

What we have discovered...is that leadership is not the private reserve of a few charismatic men and women. It is a process ordinary people use when they are bringing forth the best from themselves and others.
—**James Kouzes and Barry Posner**
The Leadership Challenge

Management works in the system. Leadership works on the system.
—**Stephen R. Covey**

Management is doing things right; leadership is doing the right thing.

—Peter Drucker

Leaders are important, but managers are the bedrock of a great organization.

—Tom Peters

Managers cope with change. Leaders cause it.

—John Kolter

Chapter 1
CONCERN
It all starts with a vision.

Remember, some people are in leadership positions while many more are in positions of leadership. What motivates a person to seek a position of leadership and then from that position take advantage of opportunities before them? What encourages a person to step into a position of leadership? Simple: It's *care for or interest in someone or something*. That's the dictionary definition of the word *concern*, and countless leadership endeavors begin there. Check it out: Most actions or endeavors all begin when some man or some woman become concerned about something.

If you trace the history of most organizations, you'll inevitably read about the time when a particular person had a vision of what could happen. Perhaps a person or a group became weary of the status quo and decided to do something about it. There's a better than excellent chance they had little or no backing or resources and few if any followers, but that never deterred them from envisioning what could be done and thus concluded they were going to be an agent for change. Leadership begins with a vision—a concern—for what could be.

A number of years ago I had the opportunity to speak at a fund raising banquet for a private school in the Midwest. In order to assist me with my remarks, I studied the history of the school. I found out that approximately 50 years before that banquet a husband and wife along with one other couple decided there was a need in the community for such a school. The next year they began the school in their garage, of all things, with a student body that consisted of their children and a few neighborhood youngsters. I was greatly impressed when I was there. The school now had 1,200 students and fantastic facilities. Where did all of this come from? How did it get started? Answer: A man and a woman saw a need, recognized and took advantage of a position of leadership and acted on their concern. What are you concerned about?

In the Old Testament of the Bible, the story of Nehemiah is about a man employed in the winter palace of the most powerful man in the world, the King of Persia. Nehemiah had a comfortable and important position and a solid relationship with his boss—the king with a funny name, Artaxerxes. Nehemiah possessed a terrific work environment ... great food and drink, a key to the royal kitchen and a position that assured his hands always being clean. However, one day he was speaking with men who had just returned from Jerusalem and he asked them about the conditions there. His peace and comfort were disrupted when they informed him that after 70 or more years the walls of the city were still in a state of utter disrepair. Nehemiah was deeply moved by this shocking news and began to cry. He immediately dropped to his knees in prayer and began fasting. Here was a man who was deeply concerned about a situation that was almost 1,000 miles from where he lived.

A lot of people knew about the walls. Many saw the problem firsthand and others no doubt stepped over and around the rubble every day. There were others who had even made attempts at restoring them but failed. Despite all of that, Nehemiah was still bothered about the city with no walls and decided something had to be done about it. This is an excellent story about a man who will eventually spearhead a miraculous and herculean task that resulted in walls being restored in 52 days. Guess where it all began? Some man in a place called Shushan had a tremendous concern about a situation in a place called Jerusalem. What are you concerned about?

I recall hearing about a professional golfer, winner of a major tournament, who was mysteriously competing in fewer and fewer tournaments. When questioned about it, he stated that he had become concerned about being an absentee dad and husband. He was running around the world, not being home to assist his wife and missing out on what was going on in his sons' lives. I guess you could say he was concerned about being a better dad and so did something about it. What a lesson to his sons. What are you concerned about?

Look around. Is there a spot just for you, a place where you are needed, a position with your name on it? Perhaps it's something you have noticed, even talked about. It's even possible you've heard yourself mention that it's too bad no one does anything about it. Why not jump in, take charge and make it happen? Stop believing it's too late, that you're not good enough, you're too old, not smart enough, or it's always been like that. Act on your concern for the thing you have been talking about and disturbed about for a long time. Stop waiting for someone to come along and fix it. What's stopping you from being that person?

It's also possible that you need to take some action from your position of leadership. There are things you have noticed—things that have bothered you—that need some supervision or some leadership. From your position of responsibility you are in an excellent place to begin working on the things that need to be altered in your business, department or family. You've seen the need. You have even spoken about the problems that should be rectified or the changes that should be made. You are in the proper position to do something about it. Act on your concern. Step up to the plate and make it happen.

Nehemiah was not in a leadership position, but there was a potential position of leadership staring at him. What he thought about doing would not be easy and there was no one to help him or encourage him, but he began to respond to the concern that was laid on his heart.

The first thing he did was pray, hoping this would help him determine the origin of his concern. He finally became convinced that the vision he had of repairing walls many, many miles away had come from God. He prayed, thought it through, examined his motives, considered the obstacles and cost, and concluded he must do something about this concern that would not go away. With a sincere heart he looked for the opportunity to act on that concern. Despite all the countless barriers, impediments and obstacles, he knew what he must do.

In a matter of months this man would lead a group of total strangers in repairing a wall that had been broken down for over 70 years. No one would have given him any chance of succeeding at that knowing his position, his relationship to the King of Persia, and where he was geographically. It is a reminder that we can never underestimate the man or woman acting on a genuine God-given concern. What are you concerned about?

As I view my life and the people around me, I think I know the things that prevent us from acting on our concerns. I think all of us can recall when we had our concerns and gave consideration to jumping in, only to stay on the sidelines. We went on thinking something needed to be changed and wondered why someone didn't fix it while all the time doing nothing ourselves. Why is that? What prevents people from their leadership positions or potential positions of leadership from responding to a situation that could be rectified if they would only do something?

Perhaps the greatest obstacle to acting on our concerns is selfishness. We are by nature self-centered people. If I am honest, I consider myself more important than you. And my comfort, my desires, my plans, and my situation take precedent over any concerns I have observed, spoken about or considered. It's equally as true that when I am wrapped up in me I even fail to notice situations that should arouse concern. Selfishness.

It's often our own shortsightedness that prevents us from initiating a course of action surrounding something that has bothered us for a long time. It would have been easy for Nehemiah to conclude that nothing could be done about the thing which concerned him. He could have easily concluded that the problems were too many, the cost too great, that someone had already tried to do that, that it's always been like that, and even though it bothered him, there really wasn't anything that could be done. After all, who was he? Shortsightedness.

Plain and simple laziness also plays a hindering role in failing to initiate something that concerns us because doing so will no doubt take some effort. Too many people feel they have already paid their dues. They don't like to be inconvenienced and they really aren't fond of what it will take to complete the task. Hard work.

Nehemiah had a nice job. He rubbed shoulders with the king and queen, was respected, lived in a palace, and held an enviable position. He lived in a rather plush, secure environment. Yes, he was concerned about the walls of Jerusalem, but to act on that concern would disrupt all of his security. A lot of us have our lives in order and we have routines that practically guarantee our peace and comfort. About the time we consider acting on a concern we have, we realize the cost to the security we so love. Security.

What are you concerned about, and what is preventing you from doing something about it?

Anything that ever resulted in a need being met, a problem being solved, or in something getting repaired originated in the heart of a man or woman who was concerned. Organizations and institutions have all sprung forth as a result of someone's concern. Read the history of your family, your school, your company or your church.

The Salvation Army serves in 118 countries today and began when a minister became concerned for the poor, the hungry and the destitute. We are all familiar with the disaster relief efforts of the American Red Cross, an organization that began in 1881 because of the concern of a single nurse from Oxford, Massachusetts, who dodged bullets during the Civil War to care for the wounded. Likewise, the destroyed walls of Jerusalem were rebuilt 2,500 years ago because of the concern of a cupbearer.

William Booth, Clara Barton and Nehemiah are illustrations of individuals who were never hired, were never presented with a job description, and who never discussed salary and benefits. They had little or no experience tackling what they took on. They simply saw what needed to be done, took advantage of a position of leadership without seeing it as such ... and the rest is history.

There is an excellent possibility you presently find yourself already in a leadership position and there is a state of affairs that needs attention. You've noticed it, walked by it, talked of it and thought about it. What are you waiting for? There is an even greater likelihood that you are close to a position of leadership. You perhaps have never thought of it that way because you haven't acted on any of the opportunities that concern you. What are you waiting for?

———————————<>——————————

Elizabeth, her husband and two children are actively involved in a local church in their small, quaint Midwestern town. Her husband is a college professor, she a stay-at-home mom and adjunct faculty member at the same university.

Elizabeth had a desire to see their church family more involved in their small community and frequently thought about and discussed ways that could happen. She always wished the church could create something that would send a message to the people of the city—especially the children—that their church was interested in them and genuinely cared. Coincidently, it was about this same time that someone pointed out to her that the church actually had a surplus of unused space. This got Elizabeth to thinking and dreaming about an after-school program that would involve and excite children. Her husband encouraged her to move ahead with her vision of bringing people together and creating a place where children could exercise their gifts and have a renewed sense of purpose. It would be a church-sponsored program that would involve others from the congregation and reach into the community so the people of that small city could view up close a group of concerned Christians.

With this vision on her heart and her goals outlined, she approached the church leadership with a plan. At first she heard many of the typical questions, Who? Where? When? How much? One of the largest questions she was delighted to address was, Why? There was even a hint of the ever popular, We've never done that before.

Finally, Elizabeth got the green light on an after- school art program for the children of the community. Word began to leak out and she was pleasantly surprised by the reactions she received from people who wanted to know more about it and who wanted to volunteer their time and offer their assistance. Parents wanted to know how they could help. Many retired teachers inquired as to how they could assist. They wanted to feel useful again, and many of them went back to files they had not been in for years and consequently were able and willing to provide much of the needed supplies.

Elizabeth had a modest goal of 20 children between ages 6-12. She ended up with 23 in the early classes and was forced to create a waiting list. Over 15 adults volunteered along with students from the two colleges located nearby. Even Elizabeth was surprised by the enthusiastic response. And as far as reaching out to the community, only 8 of the children in the earlier sessions were from families from the church.

If you could go by that church some Monday night, you would see children diligently at work with a volunteer adult standing with them and encouraging them. The word has gotten out and is spreading quickly as others want to know how they can get involved. The church staff and the church family are delighted about this effort that is connecting the church with the community.

How was all of this possible? How did it happen? Simple. A young lady in no official leadership position had a vision, a dream of something positive that could take place. With pure motives and operating within the system, she stepped into a position of leadership that is really making a difference.

See what I mean? Concern.

—————➤●◄—————

Upon graduating from the University of Missouri, Larry began working successfully in sales and marketing. Later his entrepreneurial spirit took over and he started his own firm. His wife Marilyn worked with him, overseeing the wholesale marketing operations. They worked long, hard hours in a business that was intense and exhausting and things went well. Fourteen years later they sold their company to a Fortune 500 company. Taking advantage of their now lucrative position and newfound freedom, interestingly enough, Larry and Marilyn took many months just traveling to various Bible conferences in different parts of the country.

Over the years Larry and Marilyn had simultaneously owned large homes in Michigan (one over 7,000 square feet), and they have since forgotten how many cars they once owned. They also owned a gorgeous home at Boca Grande, an island off of Florida. One day they were at that home eating lunch on their deck near the gulf. It was a beautiful day and that morning Marilyn had enjoyed a round of golf. Larry, who had played a lot of golf while in the business world and once belonged to numerous country clubs, had spent his morning fishing since he had now become an avid sport-fisherman. Here they were, living their dream after many years of exhausting work, taking advantage of the fruits of their labor. Life was good!

As they tell the story now, it was right about that time on that sun-drenched deck that they looked at each other with strange expressions. Marilyn broke the awkward silence when she said something like, "I'm so unhappy. I feel so unfulfilled. What are we doing?" Larry later said, "...as we began to talk we realized that—although we had not talked about it—we were both choking on pleasure with no purpose in life, while there were so many needs all around us."

Talk about a life-altering conversation! Driven by a deep sense of concern for their lives and a concern for the many hurting people, Larry and Marilyn decided to make some drastic changes. They immediately put both of their homes on the market and concluded they would seek ways to involve their lives with those less fortunate in the place where the home did not sell. Their beautiful, spacious home in Florida sold in 45 days, so, true to their word, Larry and Marilyn began looking for a place to make a difference. They started volunteering at the Detroit Rescue Mission, Marilyn working with women in a drug treatment center and Larry involving his time with at-risk youth. Fresh out of corporate America and right off their deck in sunny Florida, this couple began to experience firsthand the reality of having their hearts broken by the poor and disadvantaged.

Fast forward to today. Larry and Marilyn now head up a ministry they started in 2005 in the inner city of Detroit called LifeBUILDERS.[1] They have purchased homes and apartments and are ministering into the lives of men, women and children to help them reclaim lives and neighborhoods from negative influences. They labor tirelessly to supply a place where people in transition and those experiencing great need can find help reaching their goals. Their organization is supplying help, encouragement, instruction, transportation, employment and guidance in a Christian community.

One day a couple named Larry and Marilyn were sitting on their deck at their beautiful home in Florida; the next day they are doing all they can to bring hope to those less fortunate. Years before, they walked away from a leadership position and now they have taken up a position of leadership. The work is difficult, the disappointments are many, the challenge to sustain is sometimes overwhelming, but they are experiencing a fulfillment, satisfaction and just enough victories to help keep them going. LifeBUILDERS is making a difference and it is because two people responded to a concern God laid on their hearts. May their tribe increase.

See what I mean? Concern.

Concern
Motivating and inspiring quotes from others

The empires of the future are the empires of the
mind.
—Winston Churchill

*The most pathetic person
in the world
is a person who has sight,
but has no vision.*
—Helen Keller

Dissatisfaction and discouragement are not caused
by the absence of things but the absence of vision.
—Anonymous

A leader has the vision and conviction that a dream
can be achieved. He inspires the power and energy
to get it done.

—Ralph Lauren

Determine that the thing can and shall be done and then we shall find the way.
—Abraham Lincoln

There's a way to do it better. Find it!
—T. A. Edison

What is most necessary for understanding divine things is prayer.
—Origen of Alexandria

The first thing leaders should do is, sadly, the last thing many leaders actually do. The single most important thing leaders should do is pray.

—Henry Blackaby

The chief purpose of prayer is that God may be
glorified in the answer.
—**Reuben Archer Torre**

He who wants anything from God must approach
Him with empty hands.
—**Robert C. Cunningham**

The most powerful weapon
on earth
is the human soul
on fire.
—**Ferdinand Foch**

There is no other method of living piously and justly
than that of depending upon God.
—**John Calvin**

God will do nothing but in answer to prayer.
—**John Wesley**

The self sufficient do not pray…they talk to themselves. The self satisfied do not pray…they have no knowledge of their need. The self righteous cannot pray…they have no basis on which to approach God.
—Cyril J. Barber

Pursue one great decisive aim with force and determination.
—Karl von Clausewitz

You have no idea the numbers of people that God may want to influence through you. You may be perfectly positioned to influence the world because you are careful with that trust.
—Andy Stanley

How much we care depends somewhat on our estimate of the need for our caring.
—Robert K. Greenleaf

Charity is a supreme virtue, and the great channel through which the mercy of God is passed on to mankind. It is the virtue that unites men and inspires their noblest efforts.
—Conrad Hilton

Blessed is the leader who seeks the best for those he serves.
—Unknown

People can sense how you feel about them. They can tell the difference between leaders who are using them for their own gain and those who want to help people succeed.
—John Maxwell

When you set yourself on fire, people love to come and see you burn.
—John Wesley

How wonderful it is that nobody need wait a single moment before starting to improve the world.
—Anne Frank

The very essence of leadership is that you have a vision. It's got to be a vision you articulate clearly and forcefully on every occasion. You can't blow an uncertain trumpet.
—Theodore Hasburgh

When God puts a burden on your heart—get ready to be taken outside your comfort zone.
—David Hodge

The first basic ingredient of leadership is a guiding vision. The leader has a clear idea of what he wants to do–professionally and personally–and the strength to persist in the face of setbacks, even failures.
—Warren Bennis

Passion will move men beyond themselves, beyond their shortcomings, beyond their failures.
—Joe Campbell

Each one of us has a fire in our heart for something.
It's our goal in life to find it and keep it.
—Mary Lou Retton

Nothing is really lost by a life of sacrifice; everything
is lost by failure to obey God's call.
Henry P. Liddon

Never be afraid to trust
an unknown future
to a known God.
—Corrie ten Boom

Outstanding leaders go out of the way to boost the
self-esteem of their personnel. If people believe in
themselves, it's amazing what they can accomplish.
—Sam Walton

Knowing where to lead people is not the same as
convincing them to follow you.
—D.H. Everett

Chapter 2
COMMITMENT
Putting legs to your concern.

If you lived in Jerusalem during the period of time when the walls were in ruins, it is possible you walked past the rubble on a frequent basis. Suppose one day you found yourself near all the debris that had formerly been walls. You spot organized groups of people making rapid progress in rebuilding that which you always saw as muddled chaos. If you are the least bit curious, you might inquire about what is happening. No doubt, your informer would point out the man responsible for everything you were observing. And if you asked about him specifically, there is a great possibility you would have been told, "I've never seen a man so concerned about something."

The story of Nehemiah in the Bible is about the walls of Jerusalem that had been broken down for over 70 years and were amazingly rebuilt in 52 days. Why? Because one unheralded individual who was not in a leadership position acted on the concern in his heart and took hold of a position of leadership that was there for the taking.

Good leaders act with hearts of concern for a task that needs attention as well as a concern for the people who will benefit from the effort. Nehemiah's outstanding leadership in this project did begin with a genuine concern, but he's going to quickly discover it will take more than that.

You see, Nehemiah lived in Shushan and served as a domestic in the employ of a ruthless demagogue. Although Nehemiah felt compelled to act on the concern he was convinced God had laid on his heart, the possibility of that actually happening was something else. What he was concerned about was many, many treacherous miles away. He probably knew no one there and none of them knew him. I don't know if he knew anything about building walls, and besides, there was no way the king would release him from his duties in order to act on his concern. How would he travel there safely? Where was the money coming from? Where would he get the necessary materials? Besides, the task of rebuilding walls was enormous – what if he failed? There were more reasons for Nehemiah not to act on his concern than there were for him to attempt to make it happen.

Author J.I. Packer in his writings on the story of Nehemiah summed up the cupbearer, wall-builder wanna-be's predicament this way:

> *"For Nehemiah, the royal cupbearer, to be released from his job and dispatched to Jerusalem on a city building mission would be an unprecedented marvel... What he was praying for, humanly speaking, was so unlikely as to be virtually impossible."* [1]

What are you concerned about? Even though many find

a potential position of leadership staring them in the face, something they are concerned about or perhaps have been praying about, nothing happens because of the obstacles. Be comforted. You are not alone. No one had more impediments than Nehemiah.

So what did it take for Nehemiah to succeed in the midst of the obstacles? The dictionary would call it *an agreement or pledge to do something; to engage oneself with no reservations*. The word is good, old-fashioned *commitment*.

His commitment became the legs to his concern. It is one thing to have a concern. Many people talk about what needs to be done, using terms like 'if only…' or 'one of these days…' or 'it's too bad someone doesn't…' or better yet, 'I would do that myself except...'

Commitment is difficult to find in our society today. Think about how hard it is to find people who will follow through on what they have said or promised. Unfortunately, you see it in all walks of life, whether in friendships, marriages, or contractual agreements. The leader God looks for begins to emerge when he is concerned and stirred up over something and then becomes totally committed to seeing it through.

A number of months passed before Nehemiah was able to act on his concern. If you were privy to his plans, you easily could have concluded he had shelved the entire idea because of inactivity or little or no progress regarding his stated concern. The timing of action is important. Nehemiah became sensitive to God's timetable, and through prayer and counsel balanced perfectly the desire to run and make something happen quickly versus plugging into God's timetable and patiently waiting on Him.

Even though I implore you to seize the position of leadership that stares at you, don't forget the importance of timing. The balance of making it happen or going for it versus waiting on God is tricky. Some people desiring to act on their concern need to slow down and wait, while others need to stop procrastinating and go do what they said they were going to do.

It's important to notice that all the time Nehemiah waited he was nonetheless working on his goal. The opportunity finally presented itself for him to discuss his concern about the walls with the only man who could release him from his responsibilities. That conversation indicates that during the 3½ months of seeming inactivity, Nehemiah had never ceased thinking about how he could accomplish what he hoped to do when he was free to do so.

During his eventual and inexplicable conversation with the king, it became clear that Nehemiah had put a lot of thought into his vision and had begun to establish definite and specific goals. He had thought about the problem of travel through treacherous territory where he could gather needed supplies, and he had identified the individuals who could lend a necessary hand. He did all of this while waiting for the exact moment—the perfect time to make a move.

Our wall builder was able to do all of this without breaking any laws. Too often, people in their haste to do 'what God has called them to do' will run ahead of God and break many of His laws in order to accomplish His will. Nehemiah would have none of that, and it serves as a reminder to those of us who are anxious to carry out what we believe God is directing us to do. Nehemiah does not break God's law, nor does he go against the wishes of the temporal leadership of the land.

Be careful. If you are going to conclude that leadership is based on who someone is and what he or she has accomplished, there could be the temptation to accept any and all courses of action. Fans of certain causes tend to do this and are prone to applaud an accomplishment, giving credence to the adage that the ends justify the means. It seems that Nehemiah had a clear understanding of Solomon's words:

> "The king's heart is in the hand of the Lord. Like the rivers of water; He turns it wherever He wishes." [2]

Avoid the temptation or the advice from well-meaning friends to convince yourself that God has any part in law-breaking, whether His law or the law of the land, in order to accomplish His will.

Accomplishing something begins with a concern.

When that is accompanied with a strong commitment to follow through, exciting things happen.

What are you concerned about? How long have you been talking about it? When are you going to make it happen? Perhaps staring you in the face is the perfect position of leadership … why not go for it?

A group of people in England were concerned about living free in a new world. They talked about it for a long time and dreamed about what that would look and feel like. To accomplish that would be a courageous fete. Finally, on September 6, 1620, a group of 101 acted on their concern and demonstrated their commitment by stepping on a little boat called the Mayflower. After a grueling 66- day trip marked by rough seas, disease and 2 fatalities, that tiny ship—no more than 100 feet long and 25 feet wide—dropped anchor on the inside of the hook tip of what is now Cape Cod, Massachusetts.

John Kennedy was committed to landing a man on the moon. Mahatma Gandhi was committed to a free and independent India. Dwight L. Moody was committed to starting a Bible institute. Mother Theresa was committed to the poor of India. George Washington Carver was committed to assisting the people with the most needs, and America's founding fathers had a goal of freedom from foreign oppression.

Frank Staus was concerned about the youth in his community. He was committed to starting little league baseball and was laughed at because he wanted to build a field in what was a swamp. How do I know this man and this story? Because my dad waded through that swamp with him and helped him transform it into a beautiful baseball field, and I played for Mr. Staus at age 11 on that transformed swamp proudly wearing my Aston Lion's uniform. Frank Staus, an uncelebrated man with a concern and a commitment, took advantage of a position of leadership.

Leadership is not who you are and what you do – leadership is how you do it. It all begins with a God-given concern for something that needs attention, but it must be accompanied by a commitment to see it through. Translation: Leadership is a vision accompanied by definable goals.

What are you concerned about? What's preventing you from translating your seemingly impossible vision into reality?

—➤●◄—

Thom lived in a small community on the east coast and was very active in his church. He had a heart for the youth of the city and often reminded the church youth director that he was willing to assist him any time he was looking for help. The youth director told Thom he appreciated the offer and in the same conversation shared his dream of having the church reach out to attract the youth of the community who were unchurched. Thom heartedly agreed.

Thom put some thought into that vision and one day suggested that perhaps the church could sponsor a basketball league and invite the kids in the surrounding area to participate. The youth director, who was not necessarily into sports, was cool to the idea, but the more Thom thought about it, the more excited he became by the prospect of having something like that actually happen.

Unfortunately, it seemed that each time Thom talked about his goal the listener was aware of a reason it would not work. The first person questioned where the league would be held because the church gym was far too inadequate. Another person addressed liability issues in case someone got hurt. Someone else questioned how many people it would take to make it happen and where were they going to come from. One person mentioned that if it was a good idea someone would have thought of it by now. And someone else wondered how much it would cost and where was he going to get the money.

One person who had lived there a long time and claimed to know a lot of the kids questioned whether anyone would respond to the idea. Since Thom was new to the community, this observation concerned him most because he assumed the opposite. The majority of the community youth would solidly respond to such an endeavor, wouldn't they? He decided to put this question to a test and once and for all prove that particular naysayer wrong. One day he found himself standing next to a young man about 14 years of age waiting to cross the street. Thom said hello and asked, "Excuse me, I was wondering that if there was a basketball league formed in town for guys your age, would you be interested in participating?" As Thom waited for the answer that would prove his concern to be correct, he was shocked when the youth said, "Not particularly. I don't like basketball. And for that matter, neither do most of my friends." Whoops!

The young man's response was a little discouraging, but Thom couldn't help believe he was really on to something and this concern he had for the youth of the community would not go away. He decided he was not going to give up on the idea but rather commit himself even more to seeing this dream realized, regardless of the numerous obstacles he was encountering.

After thought and prayer and despite the objections he heard, Thom moved ahead with his idea. Some men in the community came alongside him, volunteering to help organize, coach and referee. As word got out about their plans, the youth of the church and the community began to respond. A league was formed, teams were organized, and a date was selected to get things rolling.

Before the first game, however, many things needed to be accomplished. Players had to be enrolled, teams and coaches selected, rules and policies established, and calendars cleared. Was it possible to play the games at the church gymnasium? To do so would be a tremendous financial advantage, but there were even obstacles there that needed to be addressed. Believe it or not, on one side of the court the out-of-bounds was a wall and on the other side was a wrought iron fence. The gym's ceiling was so low that special rules had to be instituted in case a high-arching shot hit it. There was also no scoreboard, so that too needed to be addressed.

In spite of these challenges, the commitment on the part of the leadership would not let the idea go away, so each Saturday morning a large number of local teens made their way to the small, inadequate church gymnasium to be a part of a basketball league that looked as though it had no chance to start, let alone succeed.

But it happened! And the results were fantastic. Prayer was offered just before each tip off and an air of excitement and good clean competition prevailed each morning. Coaches began building into the lives of the players. Each player was informed of all the church youth group's activities, and the youth program saw an increase in attendance.

It all happened because of someone acting on his concern and being so committed to it that no obstacle was allowed to infiltrate the heart of a person committed to doing what he felt he was suppose to do.

Thom, who helped orchestrate the league, moved unexpectedly from the community the next year. Another person just as committed stepped in, and that basketball league lasted for over 25 years. Thousands of teens from that area—boys and girls alike—participated.

See what I mean? Commitment.

COMMITMENT
Motivating and inspiring quotes from others

Vision
without a task is only a dream.
A task without a vision is but drudgery.
But vision with a task is
a dream fulfilled.
—Anonymous

Encourage your people to be committed to a project rather than just be involved in it.
—Richard Pratt

Commitment is the enemy of resistance, for it is the serious promise to press on, to get up, no matter how many times you are knocked down.
—David McNally

The quality of a person's life is in direct proportion to their commitment to excellence, regardless of their chosen field of endeavor.
—Vince Lombardi

Commitment is to engage oneself with no reservations.
—Unknown

Leadership is the capacity to translate vision into reality.
—Warren Bennis

You can't lead without taking risks.
—Andy Stanley

Unless commitment is made, there are only promises and hopes... but no plans.
—Peter Drucker

Confidence is the feeling you have
before you understand the situation.
—Unknown

You don't have to be a fantastic hero to do certain
things—to compete. You can be just an ordinary chap,
sufficiently motivated.
—Edmund Hillary

I can't imagine a person becoming a success who
doesn't give this game of life everything he's got.
—Walter Cronkite

God doesn't call the equipped.
He equips the called.
—Unknown

Visionary people face the same problems
everyone else faces; but rather than get
paralyzed by their problems,
visionaries immediately commit themselves
to finding a solution.
—Bill Hybels

Leaders are made, they are not born. They are made
by hard effort, which is the price all of us must pay to
achieve any goal that is worthwhile.
—Vince Lombardi

God places the heaviest burden on those who
can carry its weight.
—Reggie White

Anyone can dabble, but once you've made
that commitment, your blood has
that particular thing in it, and it's very hard
for people to stop you.
—Bill Cosby

You have to put in many, many, many tiny efforts that nobody sees or appreciates before you achieve anything worthwhile.
—Brian Tracy

If God sends us on strong paths, we are provided strong shoes.
—Corrie Ten Boom

Defeat is not the worst of failures. Not to have tried is the true failure
—George E. Woodberry

Dreams grow holy put into action.
—Adelaide Proctor

Chapter Two - Commitment: Putting legs to your concerns.

The greatness of a man's power is the measure of his surrender.
—William Booth

Greatness is not a function of circumstance. Greatness, it turns out, is largely a matter of conscious choice and discipline.
—Jim Collins

Never give in, never give in … never, never, never, never – in nothing great or small, large or petty, never give in except to convictions of honour and good sense.
—Winston Churchill

Vision without action is merely a dream. Action without vision just passes the time. Vision with action can change the world.
—Joel Barker

I don't care how much power,
brilliance or energy you have,
if you don't harness it and focus
it on a specific target and hold
it there, you're never going to
accomplish as much
as your ability warrants.
—**Zig Ziglar**

If there had been no fear of failure, neither would
there be any joy in success.
—**Paul Tournier**

The kind of commitment I find among the best
performers across virtually every field is a single-
minded passion for what they do, an unwavering
desire for excellence in the way they think and the
way they work.
—**Jim Collins**

Leaders often mistake compliance for commitment.
—Henry Blackaby

The relationship between commitment and doubt is by no means an antagonistic one. Commitment is healthiest when it's not without doubt but in spite of doubt.
—Dr. Rollo May

Go confidently in the direction of your dreams. Live the life you have imagined.
—Henry David Thoreau

The impossible is what no one can do until somebody does.
—Unknown

You can be anything you want to be, if only
you believe with sufficient conviction and act in
accordance with your faith; for whatever the mind
can conceive and believe, the mind can achieve.
—Napoleon Hill

Dreaming instead of doing
is foolishness.
—Ecclesiastes 5:7

Chapter 3
COURAGE
Good! You acted on your concern.
Now watch out!

Ready to lead? Warning: proceed with caution! I have been reminding you that some of us are in leadership positions while almost all of us, if we look around, are surrounded by positions of leadership. Another way of saying the latter is that masses of people are in a position to take on the leadership of something if they so desire. Many are already doing that quite well, but they do not see it as leadership because of the misconceptions discussed earlier. Unfortunately, however, too few take advantage of the frequent occurrences that call for leadership and as a result, families suffer, opportunities are missed, and needs that abound never receive attention.

One of the reasons needs that have been obvious to many for a long time go unaddressed is because of the difficulty of the task. We might admire what another is doing, but we cannot envision ourselves putting out all that effort. To dive into a situation that calls for a voice of leadership will no doubt present hassles and hard work. Too few are willing to engage themselves, knowing probable nuisances await them.

From his position of leadership Nehemiah jumped with both feet into a wall building project far away from where he lived. Everything went well at first, and all the early signs indicated he would be able to satisfy the vision he had. Amazingly, the king granted him permission to go. He had received a letter of safe travel for the trip and was given the name of the man who could assist him with supplies. When he got to Jerusalem, the people listened to him, bought into his plan and agreed to assist him with the undertaking. All of this was too much to imagine. It almost looked too easy.

Nehemiah was about to learn that good work seldom goes forward without opposition. When you wrap your concern and commitment around a project, you can almost count on someone opposing you. Just when Nehemiah and those working with him got the project off the ground, voices of disagreement, discord and antagonism began to appear.

The actual wall building effort is recorded in the Old Testament book of Nehemiah, chapter 1 through verse 15 of chapter 6. When you read the story, you will find the description of those attempting to thwart the effort in every one of those chapters but 1 and 3. The opponents of the wall building effort used every tactic to foil and discourage Nehemiah and those who had joined him in the effort. One day they would ridicule, the next day they would try mocking. When that didn't work, they resorted to deceitful tricks, then slander, and finally anger and threats.

When you step into a position of leadership, you can almost count on someone being there to criticize what you are doing and how you are going about it. The names attached to the voices of criticism for Nehemiah and his friends were Sanballat, Tobiah and Geshem. They were powerful men in the community who had the ear of the people and they were united against everything Nehemiah was sure God had called him to do.

It's very possible that in the past you took the initiative to be responsible in a position of leadership and felt good about what you were doing. It could be that at first everything went along fine. But perhaps not long after that you personally felt the stings of opposition coming at you in many forms. You discovered your concern for the situation and your commitment to continue was being tested because of the voices of dissent and discouragement. It's very possible that that experience took you down the path of anger, hurt, isolation, bitterness, doubt and thoughts of retaliation. More than one person attempting to lead others in a worthy cause has felt the stings of criticism so deeply that they simply quit. They walked away and concluded they would never do that again.

The damage wrought from criticism can do strange things to you. When you started you were convinced that was exactly what you should be doing. You were certain you were right where God called you. Things started out well so you saw that as further proof that you were on the right track. And then ... it all started to unravel.

It seems to me that, even though we know better, there's something in our subconscious that says since we have prayed about this, have received confirmation from others, have seen green lights, and consequently have concluded this is what we are suppose to do, now everything should go smoothly. Yet, when we come to our senses we know that's not normally the case.

When I resided in the New York City area, I became involved in professional sports ministry. By that I mean I was given the opportunity to frequently speak at the chapel programs conducted by the area professional teams, namely the Giants, Jets, Yankees and Mets. Chapel is an attempt to supply spiritual input into the lives of the players and is quite popular among many of the athletes.

A few years later, I moved to Atlanta, GA and was invited by Baseball Chapel, Inc. to oversee the chapel program for the Atlanta Braves. I recall when the invitation came, I responded by saying I would have to think about it and pray about it, and as a result of the time commitment, I would also have to discuss it with my wife. After doing those things, I reported to those who extended the invitation that I would accept their kind request. I stepped into the role of Braves' chaplain, not realizing I would be there for fourteen years.

Over those years I had plenty of experiences I could bore you with, but none more memorable than my first day in this new position. As I thought through the responsibilities given to me, I decided that on my first Sunday and every Sunday thereafter I would make every effort to personally speak to and invite every player, manager, coach, and clubhouse guy to chapel.

I went to the stadium that first day brimming with confidence. I was thankful for this opportunity. I knew this was where I was supposed to be and could not wait to see what God was going to do through me.

When I walked into the clubhouse, the first person I saw standing at the water fountain was someone I immediately recognized. He was the pitching coach, a veteran player of the past, one of the most outstanding pitchers of his day and a member of the Baseball Hall of Fame. Even the most novice baseball fan would have recognized him.

Remembering my decision to personally invite everyone to chapel, I figured I would start with him. He watched me approach with a look that said, "What do we have here?" I introduced myself to him as the new guy with the chapel program and informed him that we would be delighted to have him attend our meeting. I was thinking that since God had made available this opportunity, certainly this man would be so happy that I had come.

I will never forget his response when he said, "What would I want to do that for?" I was so taken aback by his reaction that I couldn't think of a good answer to his question. But before I could even answer him, he had placed his finger in my chest and said, "Look here, buddy, we don't need that here. This is a baseball clubhouse, not a church." Wow! Maybe God didn't call me here. Maybe I am not the person for the job. Maybe this isn't a place where I could be used. Had I made a mistake?

I wonder if Nehemiah, who saw all the doors open for him to do what he felt certain God had called him to do, was surprised by all the obstacles and opposition he faced once he stepped into that position of leadership. Remember, just because you are doing what you feel God has directed you to do, it is no guarantee that everything will go smoothly. Not everyone was happy when a guy named Nehemiah showed up to rebuild their broken down walls. He was going to need courage to make it happen and those who followed him were going to need him to show them the way in the face of the opposition.

The enemies in the wall building story began by asking who it was that put Nehemiah in charge. They challenged the workers about the quality of work they were doing, and they even questioned the workers' motives. If you are even the slightest bit sensitive, these types of damaging accusations get to you. All of a sudden, you doubt the call you not long ago were sure about. You begin to wonder if you are capable of constructing a supportive wall, and perhaps they are right about your motives. Criticism, second guessing, challenges and charges aren't fun.

Too frequently our response to the outbursts and the questions that accompany the indictments against us is simply to quit. In fact, that is exactly what the people who worked with Nehemiah suggested. They reminded him of the great progress that had been made but collectively felt it was futile to continue. The enemy had gotten to them.

It is at a time like this that everyone looks to the leader. What will they do? How will they react? What will they say? Nehemiah had a vision of walls around the city. His goal was to see it happen and he had a plan to ensure it worked out. Believe me when I say, nothing was going to allow him to quit.

The leader got the people together to pray. He then told them of a plan that would help them succeed despite their enemies. Finally, he challenged them to remember all the good things God had done for them, all that He had enabled them to accomplish, and he challenged the people to continue trusting in God for the future. He reminded them that the faithful God of the past desired to be the faithful God of the future.

Nehemiah, the savvy leader, handled the opposition quickly. He talked to the people openly. He was thoughtful, Biblical and tactful. He avoided sarcasm and spoke only of one issue at a time.[1] The wall building continued because of the courage of the leader.

When you take on a leadership responsibility, there will be challenges. Count on it. When (not if) they come, all the followers will look to the leader for the next step. Embrace the leader who has courage in the midst of opposition.

The word *courage* means *the quality of mind or spirit that enables one to face difficulty, danger or pain with firmness and resolve*. It is not the absence of fear – it is what you do in the face of fear. Too many leaders give up and throw in the towel in the face of criticism or disapproval and cave in to their fears. Someone once said fear is the thief of dreams.

A group of people gathered to build a wall that had been an eyesore for many years. A large contingent of people criticized them for their efforts and made enough serious threats to cause the builders to rethink what they were doing. Many wanted to quit, but when they looked into the eyes of their leader, they saw a man who was not familiar with that word. Because of his courage and leadership, they kept going and did not quit until the job was finished in 52 days.

Before I finish this section, allow me to remind you that, even though we do not appreciate criticism, be assured that it can have value. Be careful not to turn a deaf ear to the criticism that might come your way. Take time to consider what you are hearing. Is there any truth to the accusations? Have you allowed blind spots to prevent you from seeing the truth in what you are hearing? Are you guilty of what is being said? Check and recheck your motives. Have you strayed from your goals and ideals? Before you defend yourself, make sure you examine yourself. There can be value in criticism, but it won't happen if your immediate response is a blind, hasty defense of your actions.

Memorable and impactful events take place when someone jumps into a position of leadership stimulated by a concern and egged on by a commitment to make it happen. Then, when any voice of criticism or opposition appears, he has the courage to continue doing what he knows he must do and does it in a way that benefits whatever or whoever elicited the concern.

What about where you are leading? Are you facing challenges or going through a difficult stretch? Have the voices of censure or condemnation materialized to impair the project and discourage your followers? When it happens, don't forget the wall builder who after examining his heart, his motives and his call rallied the people to pray, presented a plan of action in the face of the opposition, and wouldn't allow anyone to forget the great strides they were making.

As the Republican National Convention convened in Chicago, IL in the spring of 1860, it was generally agreed that the nominee emerging to represent that party in the national Presidential race against the Democrats' Stephen Douglas and other would-be candidates would be one of two men, William Seward or Salmon Chase. However, on the third ballot on May 18, 1860, a lesser known attorney from Springfield, IL incredibly won the nomination. Abraham Lincoln was on the road to becoming the 16th President of the

United States.

As Lincoln arrived at our nation's capital to be sworn in at his March 4, 1861 inauguration, he knew what was before him. He said, "I have reached this city of Washington under circumstances considerably differing from those under which any man has ever reached it. I have reached it for the purpose of taking an official position amongst the people, almost all of whom are opposed to me." [2]

Prior to taking an oath of office, severe and unjust criticism continued against him – not just from Southern sympathizers, but it also came from the Union, from Congress, from factions in his own party, and initially from within his cabinet. The press pictured him as a grotesque baboon, a third rate lawyer, a course, vulgar joker, a dictator, an ape and a buffoon.

As for those who served with him, his Secretary of State initially saw the President as well-intentioned yet totally unqualified and incompetent to run the administration and lead the country. His Secretary of the Treasury was possessed with becoming President himself and worked tirelessly to undermine everything the President did. Throughout his entire political career Abraham Lincoln was the object of jealousy, envy and malice.

This humble man came face to face with the criticism that all too often comes to those who dare to step into a position of leadership. Lincoln responded to the criticism this way, "It often requires more courage to dare to do right than fear to do wrong. He who has the right needs not fear."

Have you exercised legitimate prerogatives from your leadership position or taken hold of a position of leadership, only to discover individuals who stood ready to criticize everything you do? Welcome to leadership.

Remember, before you defend yourself, examine yourself. After you have done that, have counseled with wise people, and have concluded your motives and actions are pure, I implore you to continue toward that concern.

Don't quit! Pray!
Don't quit! Develop a plan of action!
Don't quit! Remember what has been done!

Don't forget: The best way to avoid any manner of criticism is to do nothing. Unfortunately, too many have already done that. Come on, we are going to build a wall. Grab your trowel, take charge of that section and help us make it happen.

The Holocaust Memorial in Jerusalem is called Yad Vashem. It literally means *a hand and a name, a hand to help those in need and a name to remember those who are no more.* It is located on 45 acres and receives almost 1 million visitors annually.

One of Yad Vashem's tasks is to identify and honor non-Jews who risked their lives, liberty or positions to rescue Jews from the Nazis. Over 23,000 individuals have been recognized. They are referred to as the "Righteous Among the Nations," and a designated tree-lined avenue contains plaques bearing many of their names. Visiting there you will undoubtedly recognize such names as Oscar and Emilie Schindler, Raoul Wallenberg, Lorenzo Perrone, and the Frank family of Holland. Over 1.5 million children lost their lives during that horrific time, but there would have been more except for people like the Catholic social worker in Poland named Irena Sendler.

One unassuming plaque mentions the Dutch Christian family from the little village of Haarlem, the Ten Booms. Casper Ten Boom was a watchmaker and married to Cor. They had five children. One of the children died in infancy and Mrs. Ten Boom died in 1921. Two of the children married and moved from home, leaving Casper and his two unmarried daughters, Corrie and Betsie. Casper's watch shop was in their home on Barteljarisstrat Street. From an abbreviation of the name of the street, they simply referred to the house as the 'de Beje.'

The Ten Boom girls lived a carefree life working with their father, and they were well known in the community. Casper and his daughters were always involved in charitable work, looking out for the needs of others. They had a great concern for people less fortunate and were committed to assist where they could. In 1940, the Nazis invaded the Netherlands. Soon thereafter came restrictions on life in Haarlem, especially to the Jews of the city.

In May 1942, a well dressed woman came to the Ten Boom door with a suitcase in hand. She told them she was a Jew and that her husband had been arrested and her son had gone into hiding. Occupation authorities were watching their home and she was fearful to return there. She asked them if they would help her by supplying a place to stay. Casper's words to her were simply, "In this household, God's people are always welcome."

Thus began the "de schuilplaats" or "the hiding place". For over the next two years, Casper and his two daughters began taking in refugees, some of whom were Jews, others members of the resistance movement sought by the Gustapo and its Dutch counterpart. Due to the war food was scarce. Each non-Jewish person received a ration card with which they could procure weekly coupons to buy food. Because of the number of people seeking refuge at their home, the Ten Booms built a false wall in Corrie's room and behind it created a secret room where people hid when the Nazis called. Each day was filled with taking in people, watching the streets, and acquiring provisions while attempting to act normal, yet always fearing every knock on the door. Through all the suspense and the fear of discovery the Ten Booms displayed a rare and matchless courage, all for the sake of those who were being hunted for no reason other than what they believed.

The Nazis arrested the Ten Boom family on February 28, 1944 with the help of a Dutch informant. The family was sent to prison and Casper died ten days later. Corrie and Betsy were sent to another prison and eventually transferred to the notorious Ravensbruck concentration camp in Germany. Tragically, Betsie died there on December 16, 1944. Miraculously, despite unbearable conditions and treatment, Corrie survived Ravensbruck and was released on the last day of 1944.[3]

The Ten Booms were simple people, none of them in a leadership position. They had the love of God in their hearts and eyes full of concern. When they saw a need they took on a position of leadership, and acting courageously on that concern and commitment, they were personally responsible for the safety of hundreds.

See what I mean? Courage.

COURAGE
Motivating and inspiring quotes from others

Success is not final. Failure is not fatal.
It is the courage to continue that counts.
—Winston Churchill

Fear is that little dark room where negatives are
developed.
—Michael Pritchard

When you decide to become a leader,
you have placed a bull's eye
on your back.
—Walt Wiley

Success is to be measured not so much by the position that one has reached in life as by the obstacles which he has overcome while trying to succeed.
—Booker T. Washington

FEAR:
False Evidence Appearing Real.
—Unknown

Courage is being brave enough to do what you should do even when you are afraid.
—Unknown

Fear is absolutely necessary; without it I would have been scared to death.
—Floyd Patterson

Adversity has the effect of eliciting talents which in prosperous circumstances would have lain dormant.
—Homer

To avoid criticism, do nothing, say nothing, be nothing.
—Elbert Hubbard

Courage is not the absence of fear; it is what you do in the face of fear.
—Unknown

To fear is one thing. To let fear grab you by the tail and swing you around is another.
—Kathryn Peterson

Courage is to never let your actions be influenced by your fears.
—Unknown

I have been driven many times to my knees by the overwhelming conviction that I had nowhere else to go. My own wisdom, and that of all about me, seemed insufficient for the day.
—Abraham Lincoln

The greatest mistake you can make in life is to be continually fearing you will make one.
—Elbert Hubbard

Courage is the art of being the only one who knows you're scared to death!
—Earl Wilson

Does your problem seem bigger than life, bigger than God himself? It isn't. God is infinitely bigger than any problem you ever had or will have, and every time you call a problem unsolvable, you mock God.
—Bill Hybels

You may have a fresh start any moment you choose, for this thing that we call 'failure' is not the falling down, but the staying down.
—Mary Pickford

A prime function of a leader is to keep hope alive.
—John Gardner

Optimism
is the faith
that leads to achievement.
Nothing can be done
without hope
and confidence.
—Helen Keller

History has demonstrated
that the most
notable winners
usually encountered
heartbreaking obstacles
before they triumphed.
They won
because they refused
to become discouraged
by their defeats.
—Bertie Forbes

Courage doesn't always roar. Sometimes courage is
the quiet voice at the end of the day saying,
"I will try again tomorrow."
—Mary Anne Radmacher

A man is not finished when he is defeated.
He is finished when he quits.
—Unknown

In the middle of difficulty lies opportunity.
—Albert Einstein

Fear is the thief of dreams.
—Unknown

Pity the leader who was caught between unloving
critics and uncritical lovers.
—John Gardner

Security is mostly a superstition. It does not exist
in nature, nor do the children of men as a whole
experience it. Avoiding danger is no safer in the long
run than outright exposure. Life is either a daring
adventure, or nothing.
—Helen Keller

The unexamined life is not worth living.
—Socrates

There is a certain degree of satisfaction in having the courage to admit one's errors. It not only clears up the air of guilt and defensiveness, but often helps solve the problem created by the error.
—Dale Carnegie

Before you defend yourself, examine yourself.
—Walt Wiley

He who excuses himself accuses himself.
—Gabriel Meurier

Capitalize upon criticism. It's one of the hardest things in the world to accept criticism, especially when it's not presented in a constructive way, and turn it to your advantage.

—J. C. Penny

Hold yourself responsible to a higher standard than anyone expects of you. Never excuse yourself.

—Henry Ward Beecher

Admitting your mistakes says something profound about your basic integrity as a leader.

—Bill Hybels

Chapter 4
CONSISTENCY

It's all about the heart.

Remember, leadership is not what you do and who you are. Real leadership is about how you do it. Too many leaders use and abuse their followers and take advantage of situations for their own benefit. Too many people in leadership positions today—the ones we read about, whose pictures we view, the ones with the fancy offices in the ivory towers—are motivated by greed and place their own desires and comfort over a concern for the organization and people they lead. Unfortunately, there aren't many days that go by when you don't hear about them in the news.

The reason we need to put more emphasis on how someone leads as opposed to being infatuated with who they are and what they do is because how you do something exposes the real you ... your heart. I may be impressed after hearing either from you or one of your fans about who you are or what you do, but that doesn't really explain the real you. Titles, experiences and accomplishments seldom divulge what a person is really like.

A wise man named Solomon put it this way:

"As in water face reveals face, so a man's heart reveals the man." [1]

Let me remind you who Nehemiah was and what he accomplished: He left his cushy position in the employ of the king, traveled many miles to Jerusalem and arrived as a total stranger, motivating and leading people to rebuild in 52 days something that had been broken down for 7 decades. Wow! That's great! But what do you really know about him? What is he really like? What is his heart like? You may be in awe of his success, but you really don't know much about the real Nehemiah.

If you have ever met someone who was acquainted with a person of notoriety, someone everyone knows about and has heard about, you might be prone to ask, "What is he really like?" What you are saying is, you know about them but you are admitting you do not know the 'real' person. Unfortunately, we have held someone in high esteem from afar based on who they are and what they do, only to be disappointed when we got closer.

In this chapter we will get more deeply acquainted with the leader of the wall building project, and his actions will reveal and challenge us regarding the subject of how we lead.

As a result of Nehemiah's courage, the wall building project remained on target even in the midst of the opposition that had mounted. Nehemiah encouraged the people to pray and then laid out a plan whereby the workers remained safe from the threats and were able to continue building.

About the time that issue seemed to be under control, a more serious issue arose. Many of the workers reported that they would be unable to continue in their role because they had to tend to mounting financial obligations. This occurred because they had borrowed money from their fellow Jews and now were being forced to repay the loan that contained a substantial interest charge. When Nehemiah heard of this he became angry, not just because his work force was deteriorating but also because of what the lenders had done. You see, according to the Old Testament law found in Exodus 22 and Leviticus 25,[2] no Jew was to exact usury (interest) from a fellow Jew.

Nehemiah stepped into the middle of the issue that was pitting Jew against Jew and called out those who were disrupting the undertaking. He was rather forceful with them and bluntly told them what they were doing was wrong and that they should immediately stop.[3]

Yes, the harassment the workers received from the local residents spurred on by a few powerful voices was serious and troublesome, but this matter had the potential to be even more unsettling. Issues that emanate from the inside are always more disruptive and divisive to the harmony of any endeavor, and the leader must be strong during any time that troublesome animal rears its ugly head.

I recall my college basketball days and being a part of a new program, battling to be recognized by the schools in a particular conference. Every game was a struggle as we attempted to be successful in order to gain the respect of other colleges. We fought and fought, scrapped and scrapped, and found ourselves making progress. One thing that kept us going was the fact that as a team and coaching staff we were all in it together. Our united front served as a strength.

There was one particular evening I'll never forget. It was just before a big game toward the end of the season when an issue surfaced in the locker room that threatened to tear the team apart. It was at that time I became painfully aware of the difference between facing opposition as a team versus being confronted with issues that threatened our unity. Our team survived that internal issue mainly because of our coach, our leader.

What I find interesting about the internal issue that threatened Nehemiah and the wall building effort was what happened after Nehemiah confronted those who were responsible for this unsettling and disruptive situation. The leader saw the potentially damaging results this issue could have on the project and jumped in without hesitation. As mentioned, he forcefully challenged those who were responsible for the problem. He told them they must stop doing what they were doing and surprisingly, without the slightest hesitation, they agreed to do exactly what he said. It was like they concurred with him, even though it would impact the nice scam they had produced.

Do you find that to be strange? Why would they be so

obedient to a man whose demand would cost them a lot of money? They didn't even argue with him. They confessed they were wrong, admitted that he was right and said they would stop. Wow!

That wouldn't happen today, would it? Confession and surrender do not happen too often. No one is guilty, even if caught in the act of a wrongdoing. When people are accused today, they usually deny the accusation. The problem in this story is that everyone knew what the guilty individuals were doing. It was out in the open. They were guilty. They had no defense.

But even at that, even when there is proof of guilt, not many react the way they did. When Nehemiah confronted them, they apologized, admitted guilt and said they would change.[4] Is it just me, or have you also noticed that frequently guilty parties, having no defense for their actions, will often attack their accuser?

Let's suppose a man is accused of stealing from the company where he works. All of his misdeeds are caught on camera, and when the boss confronts him and shows him the video, he knows there is no doubt that he is guilty. Did you ever notice what we are prone to do rather than confess? We attack the one who confronted us. Before we admit our guilt, we talk about the boss's unfairness, how no one at the company likes him, or we choose this time to demean him by mentioning his weight, his hairstyle, his wife's clothes, or his unruly kids. We attempt to shed bad light on our accuser before we would ever say they are right and we are wrong.

Or let's suppose a policeman stops you for speeding and your guilt is confirmed by the radar gun that clearly indicates the speed you were traveling. No question of guilt. You were exceeding the posted speed limit. Watch what you are prone to do. Believe me, it is not thanking him for protecting the safety of the others on the highway from dangerous people like yourself. No, what you are prone to do is attack the one who says you are wrong. While he is writing out your $250 ticket, all kinds of thoughts go through your mind, such as he should be out arresting real criminals, or he is only trying to reach his quota. Or you comment on his unkempt uniform, how out of shape he appears, how he is the strangest looking policeman you have ever seen … anything other than focus on your guilt.

If this is true (and it is), why didn't these Jews attack Nehemiah? How dare he tell them to stop what they were doing! Who does he think he is? What about his own flaws or shortcomings?

Coincidently, right after this incident, Nehemiah felt inclined to describe his leadership style and his relationship with those he led. His comments offer additional insight into the man Nehemiah—not the organized, instructive boss, but an actual analysis of his heart and the way he viewed his relationship to those who dared follow him.

Could it be that those he accused had observed his

own treatment of people, his own fairness and servant's heart? Therefore, as they prepared to respond to his demands in an accusatory manner, they could think of nothing to say. Perhaps their willingness to confess their wrongdoings and their failure to attack him says as much about Nehemiah as it does about them.

When Nehemiah began to describe his administration, I began first to see the heart of the man. Secondly, I saw how he went about leading others. And thirdly, I concluded his would-be accusers were defenseless.

What I am trying to say is, is it possible that Nehemiah lived a life of consistency? He wasn't perfect—no person is—but there was a balance between what he said and what he practiced. Perhaps there is no other more positive trait for a person in a leadership position or for the person who would grasp a position of leadership than to be consistent.

Isn't that the kind of person you want to follow? One who preaches fairness, hard work, determination, sacrifice, flexibility, selflessness, and a myriad of other positive traits, and then models them himself? I know that's the kind of person I will follow.

Consistency is *the agreement or harmony of parts or features to one another*. It is the balance between what someone says and what someone does. Followers look for this characteristic in their leaders, but unfortunately few ever observe it. Children look for this in their parents, constituents hope for this in their political leaders, and the guy who labors in the cubicle around the corner prays the department leader will practice what he preaches.

In describing his administration, Nehemiah stated that despite the fact that everyone in the position before him took advantage of certain privileges by making selfish demands on the people, he did not do so. The reasons he gave for this were twofold: one was because of his concern for those who labored with him, and secondly, because of his reverential fear of God.[5]

Power does strange things to individuals. Moving into a certain office, parking in a reserved spot, getting a raise, and/or being introduced as the new boss can change a person. All of a sudden you can feel you deserve more than the others. It appears that Nehemiah's predecessors had fallen into that trap and Nehemiah was letting us know he was not guilty of that.

Nehemiah knew that those before him used their position to better themselves financially. They used their position to get to know wealthy and influential people and used that as a springboard to make purchases, especially land that had the potential to be a great investment. Nehemiah made it clear that he was there to build walls and that he and his people were there for one reason and one reason only.[6]

I like this guy. I'll follow his type. He put aside the same privileges and perks that are so much an accepted part of our society today. We can only wish our present leaders would be like that. We are completely surrounded by me-first leadership, but it's like we accept that as just the way it is. I appreciate the leader who says, "That's not why I am here." I like the leader who says, "I am here for the people." Then he conducts himself in a manner that supports what he says.

Leadership is not who you are and what you do … it's how you do it.

In their voluminous book, *The Leadership Challenge*,[7] authors/researchers James Kouzes and Barry Posner reported they surveyed thousands of working people and asked this question, "What do you look for in a leader?" When they halted the exercise they had accumulated thousands of words, but only four appeared 50% or more of the time. What do you think those words were?

The words were: inspiring, forward looking, competent, and honest. Look at them closely. The word competent speaks to what you do, but the other three words have a great deal to do with how you do it. Interesting!

Wouldn't it be great to be led by some man or woman who, no matter what they say, you know beyond a shadow of a doubt that they always speak the truth? If they said it, believe it! Take it to the bank! Wow!

I wasn't raised in a Christian home. I was part of a church youth group overseen by the pastor and his wife who had no biological children. They quickly became

Chapter Four - Consistency: It's all about the heart.

115

spiritual mentors to hundreds of us and, as a typical teenager, I was influenced by what they said. Their words were often instructive to us, sometimes in the form of admonitions and exhortations. They impacted my life, but what I really observed was the fact that though not perfect they lived what they said.

My favorite U.S. President is Harry Truman. One of my choice stories concerning him was something that took place immediately after he was informed he had become President as a result of the sudden death of Franklin D. Roosevelt on April 12, 1945.

After receiving the news, Mr. Truman went to the office of his close friend who was also Speaker of the House, Sam Rayburn. Here is the advice Rayburn gave to his friend, the new President of the United States:

> *"From here on out you are going to have lots of people around you. They'll all tell you what a great man you are, Harry ... but you and I know, you ain't."* [8]

We all, especially people in positions of leadership or authority, need friends like that lest we think we are better than the ones we lead.

Nehemiah courageously addressed an internal issue among his followers and in the process revealed that what he expected of his followers he would practice himself. That, my friends, is an excellent leader.

Leadership is not about who you are and what you do.

It's all about how you go about it, how you act, react, treat and respond to others.

⟶➤●◄⟵

His name was Bill. He worked faithfully at the same company for over 30 years. He was a dedicated, loyal employee, appreciated by his employers and well liked by his coworkers. He seemed content despite his changing responsibilities and was never particularly consumed with climbing the corporate ladder. He arrived at the office each day with a smile and a great work ethic and maintained both throughout each day.

As much as Bill appreciated his job and the lifestyle it afforded him, he was more into his family which consisted of a wife and two daughters as well as his church and his friends. It seemed as though he and his friends were always searching for ways to help others. For instance, once Bill and his buddies became aware of people who needed assistance in moving, they would volunteer to help. Frequently, you would find them on Saturdays renting a truck, banding together and helping people go from one residence to another, never charging a penny. Bill used to say, "It was hard work, but in a lot of ways it was also fun and fulfilling."

You would frequently hear Bill talking about looking out for the welfare of others and the importance of giving of yourself to those less fortunate. He was by no standards a wealthy person, but he always took more than ten percent of his gross salary and used it for others and his church. He was a great guy, had a tremendous reputation, was liked by all, and was someone I knew from 350 miles away and saw about 3 times a year.

One day all of that changed. You see, Bill was my father-in-law, and unfortunately he was forced to retire from his job because of a heart attack. After a number of their friends had moved away, I suggested he and his wife consider moving across the state and live with us. I said it without a lot of thought, never believing they would take me seriously. Well, guess what? Surprisingly, my in-laws considered it a good idea, so one day they arrived at our door, moved in, and stayed with us for the next 23 years. I used to jokingly tell men, "Remember when your mother-in-law came to visit you for a weekend? My mother-in-law did that one time, but she never went home."

Bill was no longer 350 miles away; he was down the hall. I got to see him up close every day in all kinds of circumstances. He was comfortable in his own skin, always upbeat and positive. To him the glass was always half full and everything was going to be fine. The guy I had watched from afar, at Christmas and during a couple of days in the summer months, was the same guy who moved in with me.

Bill never compromised his values and in the process left an unbelievable legacy, not only to me and everyone else, but especially to his grandsons, our two sons whom he lived with. He knew that no matter what our stations in life, it is possible to make a difference in the lives of those around us, even those who live under our own roof.

The title 'Pop Pop' does not come with a job description, and I know of no one who starts receiving a salary when getting that title. But it is clearly a position of leadership from which generations can be impacted. Our two sons still talk about and quote their grandfather. They as well as my wife and I heard his consistent reminders about things that really matter, behavior that counts and reactions that make a difference. And then, of all things, we watched him practice each and every one of them. Do our two sons still remember that? You bet they do, and so does Bill's son-in-law.

Like thousands of others, Bill was in a unique, impressionable position of leadership. He never left us with a lot of money, scrapbooks full of accomplishments, associations we could take advantage of, or a bunch of stuff. In retrospect, those things seemed unimportant compared to the legacy of consistency he left behind for all of us to observe.

See what I mean?   Consistency.

CONSISTENCY
Motivating and inspiring quotes from others

One cannot do right
in one area of life
whilst he is occupied
in doing wrong in another.
Life is one indivisible whole.
—Gandhi

Without consistency
there is no moral strength.
—Owen

The secret to winning is constant,
consistent management.
—Tom Landry

In essence, if we want to direct our lives,
we must take control of our consistent actions.
It's not what we do once in a while
that shapes our lives, but
what we do consistently.
—Tony Robbins

89% of what people learn comes through visual
stimulation, 10% through audible stimulation. So
it makes sense that the more followers see and hear
their leader being consistent in action and word, the
greater their consistency and loyalty.
—John Maxwell

Without credibility,
you can't lead.
—Brian Carroll

Be a pattern to others, and then all will go well: for as a whole city is affected by the licentious passions of great men, so it is likewise reformed by their moderation.

—Cicero

Whoever is careless with the truth in small matters cannot be trusted with the important matters.

—Albert Einstein

People may doubt what you say, but they will believe what you do.

—Lewis Cass

It is easy to love the people far away.
It is not always easy to love those close to us.
It is easier to give a cup of rice to relieve hunger
than to relieve the loneliness and pain
of someone unloved in our own home.
Bring love into your home
for this is where our love for each other
must start.
—Mother Teresa

Leaders must behave the way they wish their
followers would behave.
—Unknown

One of the marks of excellent people is that they
never compare themselves with others. They only
compare themselves with themselves and with their
past accomplishments and future potential.
—Brian Tracy

Example is not the main thing in influencing others.
It is the only thing.
—Albert Schweitzer

Effective leadership is not based on being clever,
it is based on being consistent.
—John Maxwell

Y ou have to set
the tone and pace,
define objectives and strategies,
demonstrate
through personal example
what you
expect from others.
—Stanley C. Gault

Your job gives you authority.
Your behavior gives you respect.
—Irwin Federman

People struggle with life balance simply because
they haven't paid the price to decide what
is really important to them.
—Steven Covey

P eople are changed,
not by coercion
or intimidation,
but by example.
—John Maxwell

Nothing is so potent as the silent influence of a good example.
—**James Kent**

My sense of reality became distorted because of power.
—**Dick Morris**

Example has more followers than reason.
We unconsciously imitate what pleases us, and approximate to the characters we most admire.
—**Christian Nestell Bovee**

A loyal constituency is won when people judge the leader to be capable of solving their problems and meeting their needs.
—John Gardner

T here is nothing so annoying as a good example!
—Mark Twain

T here is something about being placed in a position of leadership or being in charge that can do strange things to us.
—Walt Wiley

Pride ever lurks
at the heels of authority.
Even a little authority
is prone to turn
the seemly walk
into a most
offensive strut.
—J.H. Jowett

From here on out you are going to have lots of
people around you. They'll tell you what a great man
you are, Harry…but you and I know… you ain't.
—Sam Rayburn
*Spoken to Harry Truman as Truman became
President in April 1945*

We fear men so much
because
we fear God so little.
—Unknown

Yet He is not partial to princes, nor does He regard the rich more than the poor; for they are all the work of His hands.
—Job 34:19

*P*eople fear the voice of their neighbors more than the voice of God.
—H.G. Wells

For this is the will of God, that by doing good you put to silence the ignorance of foolish men…
—I Peter 2:15

*A*dversity is hard on a man; but for one man who can stand prosperity, there are a hundred that will stand adversity.
—Thomas Carlyle

Then Peter opened his mouth and said: *"In truth I perceive that God shows no partiality."*
—Acts 10:34

CHAPTER 5
CHARACTER
It's all about the people.

The famous Dale Carnegie once said, "Dealing with people is probably the biggest problem you face, especially if you are in business. Yes, and that is also true if you are a housewife, architect or engineer." [1]

When you take on a leadership position or take advantage of a position of leadership, you are no doubt going to have to deal with people. If you can do what you feel called to do by yourself, by all means do that. But once you invite others to join you in the effort, like it or not, you have become a leader.

If Nehemiah could have rebuilt the dilapidated ruins of Jerusalem alone, he would have saved himself some headaches and heartaches, but this mammoth task meant getting many others involved.

Nehemiah had to work with people and how he went about that revealed a lot about the man and his heart. In his group of workers were complainers, slouches, prima donnas, people in high places, and a long list of quality workers. The make-up of his crew was possibly quite typical of work forces we see today.

I believe you clearly see the heart of this man when you see his consistency. He obviously practiced what he preached. However, I also believe his *character* is demonstrated in his handling of his position and his response to those he led.

In further describing his administration and his response to those who followed him, Nehemiah reminded us that he did not demand provisions as his predecessors had. The reason for that was "...because the bondage was heavy on the people." He concluded his remarks by stating, "Remember me, my God, for good, according to all that I have done for these people." [2] I told you, I like this guy.

I like the way this leader viewed the people who followed him. They were not there to make him look good. They were not there for him to abuse or take advantage of. They were seen as co-laborers who were to be protected, fulfilled, and even served.

I believe his response to those he led and the way he viewed them speaks of Nehemiah's character.

Character is *a moral or ethical quality attributed to a person*. When we are looking for a dentist, a mechanic, financial advisor, plumber or pastor, or even when we have a vote in filling a political office, we look for a person with moral and ethical quality that is above reproach.

People of character are believable; you can trust them. With them you know you are in good hands. You want to deal with organizations led by people of character. You want to do business with companies led by men or women who have character. You want to follow a person of character.

What is the most reliable way of determining a person's character? How do you know if a person is of good character or not? If you do not have the luxury of being with someone on a regular basis, what would be a sure-fire barometer of that person's character?

One of the best ways to determine an individual's trustworthiness, reliability, authenticity, genuineness or legitimacy is to observe how he or she relates to and treats people. Think about it: A person's character is best revealed, tested and sharpened in his or her relationship with people.

Isn't it possible that our children's great contribution to us is the way they are able to reveal, test and sharpen our character? Haven't you had an occasion where your teenager was able to disclose the real you? If you want to discover what a person is really like, just be around them for a period of time and watch how they act and react around others. It will reveal volumes.

If you study the most well-known Bible characters, you will note that God was concerned about how they treated people. Don't ever forget: With God it's not about such things as corporate positions or business entities, our leisure activities, or even our church attendance. God is in the people business.

The Old Testament character Joseph had every excuse to

be bitter and seek revenge against his brothers because of what they had done to him, yet when the occasion for retribution arose, you saw the real Joseph.[3]

Moses, the great leader of the people of Israel, led millions through the wilderness and they frustrated him at every turn, yet he consistently cared for them, encouraged them, and on more than one occasion spared their lives. It was as a result of those self-indulging, self-centered, complaining people that we get to see the real Moses.[4]

David, Israel's greatest king, had all the power but he was clear about using it for the benefit of the people he led.[5] When David's son Solomon inherited the throne, he pleased God when, after being told he could have anything he wanted, he asked for wisdom so he could effectively serve God's people.[6]

Don't miss it: God blessed the leaders who put people first.

Dale Carnegie had it correct. Working with people can present challenges. Ask anyone who works in retail or who deals with people on a regular basis. Individuals can be inconsiderate, insolent, incongruent and downright impossible. Notice that Joseph put the circumstances of his brothers over the temptation to be vindictive. Moses, though frustrated by those he led, was the one who went to bat for them. David confessed that the reason he was in his leadership position was for the sake of the people, not for himself. And when

Solomon could have had anything he wanted, he asked for wisdom in order to serve his people. Each of these Old Testament characters understood why they had been placed in those leadership positions.

Perhaps it was best said by Ezekiel in 34:2:

> "Woe to the shepherds of Israel who only take care of themselves."

We have been placed in a leadership position or we have grasped a position of leadership, not for our sake but for the sake of those we are privileged to lead. Sadly, most of our leadership models only give lip service to that and tragically use the people they lead for their own benefit.

After 40 years of reigning, Solomon died and his son Rehoboam ascended the throne. Shortly after that, the new king sought advice from his advisors. The younger generation advised him to seize power, clutch outright control, show the people who is in charge, and tax them even more than his father had done. The older generation suggested a more moderate approach to the new king and uttered these powerful words:

> "If you will be a servant to these people today, and serve them, and answer them, and speak good words to them, then they will be your servants forever." [7]

Janusz Korczak was born in Warsaw, Poland in 1878.

He became a pediatrician and served in both the Russo-Japanese War and World War I. With an acute interest in children—especially orphans—he began writing children's book under the pen name, Henryk Goldszmit. His books, *Child of the Drawing Room*, *King Matt the First*, and *King Matt on a Desert Island* won national acclaim.

In 1911, he became the director of Dom Sierot, an orphanage of his own design for Jewish children in Warsaw. He formed a kind of republic for the children which consisted of a parliament, a court and a newspaper written by the children. Korczak reduced his duties as doctor and served the children of the growing orphanage while living in the attic.

In 1940, the Germans created the Warsaw Ghetto and Korczak's orphanage was forced to move from their building. On August 5, 1942, German soldiers arrived to collect the 192 orphans and staff of over a dozen to take them to the Treblinka extermination camp. Dressed in their best clothes, the children marched through the street, each carrying a blue knapsack and their favorite toy. Their leader, Janusz Korcza, was out in front.

As they marched through the ghetto, eye witness Joshua Perle described the scene:

> "A miracle occurred... Two hundred children did not cry out. Two hundred pure souls, condemned to death, did not weep. Not one of them ran away. None tried to hide. Like

stricken swallows they clung to their teacher and mentor, to their father and brother, Janusz Korczak, so that he might protect and preserve them. Janusz Korczak was marching, his head bent forward, holding the hand of a child, without a hat, a leather belt around his waist, and wearing high boots. A few nurses were followed by two hundred children, dressed in clean and meticulously cared for clothes, as they were being carried to the altar. On all sides the children were surrounded by Germans, Ukranians, and this time also Jewish policemen. They whipped and fired shots at them. The very stones of the street wept at the sight of the procession."

According to legend, when the procession reached the station, an SS officer recognized Korczak as the author of one of his favorite children's books and offered to help him escape. It was also reported that Nazi authorities had in mind some kind of special treatment for the author and offered him his freedom. Whatever the offer, Korczak refused, desiring to stay with his children. And with that he marched with them to the trains taking them to their death at Treblinka.[8]

Look for the leader who has character, one you can believe and trust. To determine that, observe how they view people. Watch how they respond to people, treat people and direct people. I repeat: A person's character is best revealed, tested and sharpened in his/her relationship with people.

At 10:15 p.m. on Good Friday, April 14, 1865, Abraham Lincoln was assassinated by John Wilkes Booth at Ford Theater in Washington, D.C. There had been numerous threats on the President's life, and all of his advisors had cautioned him to be careful about where he would be seen in public. After the Lincolns notified the theater that they would be coming to see the play, *My American Cousin*, Mr. Lincoln began to think better of it. Later the President told White House security guard William Crook: "It has been advertised that we will be there, and I cannot disappoint the people. Otherwise, I would not go. I do not want to go." [9]

Remember, as long as you can manage things by yourself, that's fine. But the moment you invite someone else to join you, you become a leader. You manage checkbooks and portfolios; you lead people. You don't lead companies, departments, committees or churches; you lead people. That in itself can present problems because people can be a challenge. Some can be complex, others lazy, some can be downright obstinate, and none of them will be just like you. But be assured, those you lead will play a role in revealing, testing and sharpening your character. Through them and your relationship to them, everyone will be able to see if you are the real thing or not.

I'll never forget the time a close friend who was president of a company (a man of impeccable character) sadly had to inform his employees that the firm was being forced to close their doors. He dreaded the meeting where this would have to be presented. Miraculously, it turned out that the organization who would occupy their facility was able to offer positions to each of my friend's employees, and they would not only maintain their positions, but they wouldn't even have to move out of their building or offices. My friend delighted in the final outcome.

In discussing this further, I asked him what this meant to him and his future. He told me he was out of a job and unemployed. When I asked if he ever discussed a possible position with the new company, I'll never forget his response, "To be honest, it never entered my mind. I'm so happy because all I cared about was what was going to happen to my people."

Character is best revealed, tested and sharpened in our relationship to people.

━━━━⇒✦⇐━━━━

There were no corporate headhunters calling on her to offer her a position, a title or salary. She actually never worked outside her home, but somewhere along the way, somehow she realized she could make a difference from her unique position of leadership. She was concerned about that, totally committed to what she was doing, and exemplified unbelievable courage in the face of numerous discouragements and unbelievable heartache.

She managed to live for 73 years and is often recognized as a model of a courageous mother. She was the 25th and last child born to Dr. Samuel Annesley and Mary White. She married Samuel Wesley on November 11, 1688 when she was 19. Together they had 19 children in a span of 20 years: 9 of the children died as infants, 4 of the children that died were twins, a maid accidently smothered 1 child, and at her death in 1742, only 8 of her children were still alive.

She experienced many hardships throughout her life. Her husband left her and the children for over a year because of a minor dispute. She once told him, "I am not a man, yet as a mother I feel I ought to do more than I had yet done. I resolve to begin with my own children; in which I observe, the following method: I take such a proportion of time as I can spare every night to discourse with each child apart. On Monday I talk with Molly, on Tuesday with Hetty, Wednesday with Nancy, Thursday with Jacky, Friday with Patty, Saturday with Charles."

The family was always facing financial issues. Their house burned down twice, and during one of the fires her son John had to be rescued from the second story window and nearly died. She took charge of the education of each of the children. The day after their 5th birthday their education began, and she sternly demanded 6 hours of study per day. Each of the children learned Latin and Greek and they were all tutored in the classical studies of England. She taught the children 6 hours a day, 6 days a week, for over 20 years.

Her husband spent his entire life and the family finances on a book. His work was never recognized and had little impact other than placing tremendous financial burdens on his family.

She became disenchanted with the church they attended and decided to keep the children at home on Sunday afternoons. They would sing a psalm and then she would read a sermon. The local people began to ask if they could attend, and at one point over 200 people would attend the family 'church meeting'.

This 25th child of 25 and mother of 19 spent all her life instilling a Christian destiny into each of her children. She made known her 16 rules for raising a child including such things as no eating between meals, everyone in bed by 8, take medicine without complaining, never allow a sinful act to go unpunished, observe all promises, and teach the children to fear the rod.

She was a great believer in things such as integrity, sincerity, decency, honesty and veracity. She understood that they were characteristics one could receive from their upbringing and she quickly realized she was in a unique position to pass those traits along to her children. She respected people of moral fiber and character and desired those things for herself and each of her children.

Susanna Wesley never preached a sermon, published a famous book, founded a company or began a movement. She was hardly recognized outside her home. She simply dove into an unbelievable position of leadership with the title of 'Mom' and hoped God would use the efforts she put forth in order to impact the children He had entrusted to her. As a woman of character she labored tirelessly to instill that quality into the lives of her children. The results: She is often seen as a model mom, 3 of her sons became preachers, and, oh yes, 2 of them turned a country—yea, the world—upside down.[10]

See what I mean? Character.

CHARACTER
Motivating and inspiring quotes from others

In the past a leader was a boss. Today's leaders must be partners with their people... They no longer can lead solely based on positional power.
—Ken Blanchard
Leadership—Partnership—Power

Blessed are the leaders who seek the best for those they serve.
Beatitudes for Leaders:
—Author Unknown

Too many leaders act as if the sheep— their people—are there for the benefit of the shepherd, not that the shepherd has responsibility for the sheep.
—Ken Blanchard
Leadership—Responsibility

Circumstances do not make the man, they reveal him.
—James Allen

Leadership should be born out of an understanding of the needs of those who would be affected by it.
—Marian Anderson

The key to being a
good manager
is keeping the people
who hate you
away from those
who are still undecided.
—Casey Stengel

Good leaders make people feel that they are at the very heart of things, not at the periphery; everyone feels that he/she makes a difference to the success of the organization. When that happens, people feel centered and that gives their work meaning.
—Warren Bennis

Are you building people, or building your dream and using people to do it?
—Unknown

Reputation is what men and women think of us;
character is what God and angels know of us.
—Thomas Paine

Character is the will to do what's right,
even when it's hard.
—Andy Stanley

We are given power
not to advance our own purposes,
nor to make a great show
in the world, nor a name.
There is but one use of power
and it is to serve people.
—George H.W. Bush

Of all the properties which belong to honorable
men, not one is so highly prized as that of character.
—Henry Clay

Leadership is a potent combination of strategy and
character. But if you must be without one –
be without strategy.
—Norman Schwarzkopf

In matters of style, swim with the current; in matters of principle, stand like a rock.
—**Thomas Jefferson**

Character cannot be developed in ease and quiet. Only through experiences of trial and suffering can the soul be strengthened, vision cleared, ambition inspired and success achieved.
—**Helen Keller**

Leadership without character is unthinkable—or should be.
—**Warren Bennis**

A solid trust is based on a consistent character.
—**John Maxwell**

We must constantly strive
to keep our integrity intact.
When wealth is lost,
nothing is lost;
when health is lost,
something is lost;
when character is lost,
all is lost.
—**Billy Graham**

The greatest use of life is to spend it for
something that outlasts it.
—**William James**

Nearly all men
can stand adversity;
if you want to
test a man's character,
give him power.
—**Abraham Lincoln**

Leadership is an opportunity to serve. It is not a
trumpet call to self-importance.
—**J. Donald Walters**

True leadership must be for the benefit of the followers, not the enrichment of the leaders.
—**Robert Townsend**

He is no fool who gives that which he cannot keep to gain what he cannot lose.
—**Jim Elliot**

The true measure of a man is how he treats someone who can do him absolutely no good.
—**Samuel Johnson**

You can't live a perfect day without doing something for someone who will never be able to repay you.
—**John Wooden**

There are many qualities that make a great leader. But having strong beliefs, being able to stick with them through popular and unpopular times, is the most important characteristic of a great leader.
—**Rudy Giuliani**

Character
is not made in a crisis
– it is only exhibited.
—Robert Freeman

To lead, you have to have the trust of the players, and to do that you have to find a way to connect with them, to find a common ground with every individual. Leading is a people issue, not a sports issue.

—Mark Messier

One thing I know: the only ones among you who will be truly happy are those who will have sought and found how to serve.

—Albert Schweitzer

A great leader never sets himself above his followers except in carrying out responsibilities.

—Unknown

In free governments, the rulers are the servants and the people their superiors and sovereigns. For the former, therefore, to return among the latter is not to degrade them, but to promote them.

—Ben Franklin

And they spoke to him saying, "If you will be a servant to these people today, and serve them, and answer them, and speak good words to them, then they will be your servants forever."

—King Rehoboam's Advisors: 1 Kings 12:7

One who leads in the style of Jesus does not use forms of coercion, nor does he depend on institutional position for authority. Instead, by serving people, he leads as they recognize his ability and choose to voluntarily follow.

—Gayle Erwin

You can only get
what you want
if you help
enough other people
get what they want.
—**Zig Ziglar**

Be more concerned with your character than your reputation, because your character is what you really are, while your reputation is merely what others think you are.

—John Wooden

Character is like a tree and reputation its shadow.
The shadow is what we think it is;
the tree is the real thing.
—Abraham Lincoln

You can accomplish anything
in life, provided you
do not mind who gets the credit.
—Harry S. Truman

People are illogical, unreasonable, and self-centered.
Love them anyway.
If you do good, people will accuse you of selfish
ulterior motives. Do good anyway.
If you are successful, you will win false friends
and true enemies. Succeed anyway.
The good you do today will be forgotten tomorrow.
Do good anyway.
Honesty and frankness make you vulnerable.
Be honest and frank anyway.
What you spend years building may be
destroyed overnight. Build anyway.
People really need help but may attack you if
you do help them. Help people anyway.
Give the world the best you have and you'll get
kicked in the teeth.
Give the world the best you have anyway.

—Adapted by Mother Teresa

But Jesus called them to Himself and said to them, *"You know that those who are considered rulers over the Gentiles lord it over them, and their great ones exercise authority over them. Yet it shall not be so among you; but whoever desires to become great among you shall be your servant. And whoever of you desires to be first shall be slave of all. For even the Son of Man did not come to be served, but to serve, and to give His life a ransom for many."*
—Jesus of Nazareth:
Mark 10:42-45

Chapter 6
WHAT NOW?

Probably all of us have a list of the things we were going to do. It could be as mundane as clearing out the garage or something more meaningful like being a better husband or father. What we were going to do could certainly be classified as important, it's just that we never got around to it. Our lives are unfortunately marked by "I'm hoping to…" or "I wish I had" or sadly perhaps "it's too bad I never…" It was Henry Ford who once said, "You can't build a reputation on what you were going to do."[1]

I wrote this book to encourage and/or exhort the readers to use their established leadership positions to make a difference. Because of your appointed situation you probably have the opportunity to make something happen, fix something that needs to be fixed, or change what should not be. You know what that is and you are in the position to do it. Go for it!

I more specifically wanted to remind you the readers that you are more of a leader than you think you are. And, if you would only look around, you no doubt will discover countless opportunities of positions of leadership you can take advantage of. What have you noticed at your church that needs some attention? What could use some work in your community, at the office, or perhaps right in your own home? Why don't you do something about it? You know you have mentioned it, talked about it, or considered it. Go for it!

I want to challenge you to stop talking about a place where you can make a difference and go make a difference. Somewhere there is a situation, there is a group, there is a need, a face that is calling out to you. Don't just briefly pause, stop pondering. The time to think about it is over. I dare you to courageously respond to that voice that is saying, "Gonna need a leader here."

There are over 200 quotations in this book. Although I am fond of all of them, I believe my favorite is this one from Mark Twain:

> "Twenty years from now you will be more disappointed by the things you didn't do than by the things you did do."

If you have the opportunity and you are so inclined, please email me at **wweoffice@att.net** and let me know what concern you have acted on and what the results were.

END NOTES

Preface
[1] Parakaleo – A Greek word meaning to encourage or
    exhort
[2] Acts 8:30-31

Introduction on Leadership
[1] *Good to Great*: Jim Collins, author; published by
    Harper Business, 2001.

Chapter 1 – Concern
[1] LifeBUILDERS: *www.LifeBuildersDetroit.com*

Chapter 2 – Commitment
[1] *A Passion for Faithfulness*: J.I. Packer, Author;
    published by Crossway Books, 2001.
[2] Proverbs 21:1

Chapter 3 – Courage
[1] Nehemiah 4:13-15; 5:6-11
[2] Reply to a Serenade at Washington in *'The Complete
    Works of Abraham Lincoln, v.6'*
[3] *The Hiding Place*: Corrie ten Boom, Author;
    published by Viking Press, Inc., 1971.

Chapter 4 – Consistency
[1] Solomon: Proverbs 27:19
[2] Exodus 22:25; Leviticus 25:35-38
[3] Nehemiah 5:9-11
[4] Nehemiah 5:12
[5] Nehemiah 5:15

[6] Nehemiah 5:16

[7] *The Leadership Challenge*: James Kouzes and Barry Posner, Authors; published by Jossey-Bass, a Wiley Company, 2002.

[8] *Truman*: David McCullough, author; Part 3 – To the best of my ability: p. 440.

Chapter 5 – Character

[1] *How to Win Friends and Influence People*: Dale Carnegie, author, published by Simon and Shuster, 1937.

[2] Nehemiah 5:18

[3] Genesis 45: 5-9

[4] Deuteronomy 32:11-14; Numbers 14:11-19

[5] II Samuel 5:12

[6] I Kings 3:5-10

[7] I Kings 12:7

[8] *www.economicexpert.com*– See Janusz Korczak

[9] *www.mrlincolnswhitehouse.org*

[10] *www.kikipedia.org*– See Susanna Wesley

All Scriptures taken from the
New King James Version.

ABOUT WALT WILEY AND WINNING WITH ENCOURAGEMENT

Walt Wiley is the founder and president of Winning With Encouragement, Inc. He is a noted teacher and travels to present numerous seminars that WWE has produced. He is also a popular speaker in various venues across the country.

Winning With Encouragement, Inc. is a teaching ministry based in Charlotte, NC. WWE is a 501(c)(3) organization incorporated in Georgia and North Carolina overseen by a Board of Directors consisting of individuals in business and ministry related fields.

WWE's material is very popular in churches, at conferences, conventions, retreat centers, and wherever a group of people gather who wish to be encouraged through simple yet profound and entertaining instruction from the Bible.

WINNING WITH ENCOURAGEMENT

TEACHINGS FROM WWE:

Effectively Handling All that You Have
We all have lots of things—sometimes more than we need. That's fine, as long as we have the correct view of all that we have.

Figuring Out People Who Aren't Like You
Learn how to cope with your family members, neighbors and co-workers by better understanding them and yourself.

Finding Encouragement in a Discouraging World
A Scriptural reminder that we discover encouragement and God is pleased when we pay attention to what is important to Him.

How to Get Your Mate to be Like You...So You'll Both Be Perfect
A study of the factors that contribute to making marriage a challenge and what to do about them.

How to Encourage
An examination of the 4 methods at our disposal that are guaranteed to bring encouragement to others.

Raising Kids is a Piece of Cake
Parenting is simply preparing a child for life. Learn the ingredients that will help a parent succeed.

Standing Out in the Crowd
Learn 16 characteristics that will make you a positive contributor wherever you work with others.

The Encouragement Seminar
A study comparing what Jesus pointed out as being important and significant as opposed to what our society leads us to believe. When you see like He sees, you will be encouraged.

The Look of the Leader
A look at 5 leadership traits that produce a leader's success and the follower's fulfillment.

BIBLE LAND PILGRIMAGES:

WWE has been privileged to lead hundreds of people on pilgrimages to the lands of the Bible. These educational, entertaining, and deeply impactful ventures include trips to Israel, Greece, Turkey, Jordan and Egypt.

Learn more about

Winning With Encouragement, Inc.,

by visiting their website:
www.wweministries.org